Part I: Purpose and Vision

If you are in happiness,
If you are not in happiness,
thi...
If you do not see these things ... ...ness will escape you.
If you would be happy then you must look beyond the things that you know.
And there you will find the depths of yourself.

This is the mystery and the wonder of life.
If you are ready to see, then I can show you much.
And you will find that we are the same and of one.

Attributed to an ancient Indian Sage.

To Mac,
with love and appreciation,
Morel Fourman
February 7th 2006

FIRST EDITION
April 2005

Copyright © Morel Fourman 2000-2005.
All Rights Reserved.

Email: Morel.Fourman@gmail.com

Book of Personal and Global Transformation

Part I: Purpose and Vision

A Story: The Idea That Changed the World

Once upon a time, there was a beautiful planet.
But the beautiful planet was sad.
Wonderful and loving people lived on the beautiful planet. But they often got stressed and fearful and did things that were not very helpful. They were doing their best, but they were stressed by life and doing their work. They were stressed by lots of things they thought they couldn't change. They worked in great big organisations and little organisations. The organisations did amazing things that changed life for everyone. But the managers in the organisations were stressed and often afraid, with bills to pay and customers to look after and things to do. They often forgot to think about the people who worked for them and the world around them.

Good people worked in good organisations, but they often did things that weren't helpful and things got worse for people and the planet.

Everyone had always wanted a world that was better and fairer, so they invented society to help them to live and work together. They chose inspiring and impressive leaders and they paid taxes to make society work.

Good people were elected with big ideas to make things better.

They used the taxes to pay for government, to make the big ideas work and to make things better.

Good people worked for the Government because they wanted to make things better too.

But sometimes, the leaders got afraid that their big ideas would not work out, so they tried to make the good people who worked for the Government work better and harder.

Sometimes the leaders made the people who worked for them stressed and afraid, so they were afraid to try new things, even the ones to make things better.

The leaders were disappointed because they had such big plans to make things better.

The people who worked for them were disappointed because no one seemed to appreciate them.

The society didn't work so well because the government was doing its best, but was getting stuck. There was more stress for organisations and the people who worked in them. They had enough trouble just doing what they had to do, so they didn't have time to make things better.

The people who worked for the organisations and the governments were the same people who elected the governments. They became disappointed and said: "If governments can't change society and organisations can't change the world, then how can things get better?"

It was a good question and people talked about it a lot.

While this was going on, the planet was getting sadder and the people got more stressed and afraid.

Some people blamed the Government. Others blamed organisations and other people. That didn't really help, because whoever got blamed became defensive and afraid and they got more stressed. The more stressed they got, the less they could do! People became disappointed because they realised they couldn't make other people change.

People thought a lot about how other people could change to make things better and sometimes they blamed them when they didn't.

Eventually, someone came up with a different question that helped people to see things differently: "Who can change governments and organisations so they can change the world."

People began to realise that only people could change the government to change society and only people could change organisations to change the world, but changing people didn't turn out to be all that easy.

Some very clever people tried some very clever things, but there weren't enough clever people to go round and often the clever things didn't work without them!

Then someone had an idea that didn't seem very clever at all, but it was a good idea and the idea spread and things began to change.

The people who understood the idea began to get happier. The more they thought about it, the more they knew they could change the world and the less stressed they felt.

Other people liked them because they were happy and successful. People who understood the idea began to meet each other by accident and they started to help each other.

As the people used the idea to work together, the changes became faster and faster.

The idea was so simple that by now change was sweeping across organisations, governments and societies. The people who were using the idea became even happier and even more successful. Even in difficult times, the beautiful planet was beginning to smile because it could feel the change.

And the skies were laughing because the idea was so simple that people had been too clever to see it.

So what is the simple idea?

"If I can change myself, I can change the world!"

I. Acknowledgements

I would like to acknowledge David Bohm, Physicist, archaeologist of language and a beautiful gentle soul for his life's work which first introduced my intellect to the science of implicate order (unseen, unmanifest, as yet unexpressed) and explicate order (tangible, manifested, expressed in form). He also introduced me to the fact of unbroken pervasive wholeness in a Universe that we speak of and relate to in fragments.

Thanks for their support with this book, in order of appearance, to Graham James, Glen McCoy, Cathryn McNaughton, Gabriele Sommer, Jon Wheeler, Jodechi Giese, William Spear, Davina MacKail, Silvia Tassarrotti, Mike Griffiths, Siri Data, William Bloom, Barbara Hamilton, Gwyneth Moss and Marthe Muller. Thank you so much to my dear partner Gina Lazenby for her love and encouragement and for supporting me in every way in life.

Part I: Purpose and Vision

II. To skim this book in 30 minutes
- Relax and smile
- Read the table of contents below.
- Read the first chapter: "A time of change" on page 1
- Skim through the book reading only the headings and bold text.
- Skip plain text and grey shaded portions.
- Read "You and I make the difference" on page 106.
- Read the Summary on page 108.

III. Table of Contents

A Story: The Idea That Changed the World i
I. Acknowledgements iv
II. To skim this book in 30 minutes v
III. Table of Contents vi
IV. The journey to this book viii
V. Science, intent and consciousness viii
VI. September 11th 2001: a changing world xiii
VII. How to use this book xvi
1. A time of change 1
2. The Emerging Global Transformation 4
3. The true joy in life: serving a purpose 11
4. Vision: the tidal pull of Global Transformation 15
5. The Zen Archer: aligning with purpose 17
6. Intuition: the gift of personal guidance 19
7. Stillness: the gift of peace of mind 24
8. Reclaiming free will 29
9. Radiating love 34
10. The beautiful garden of my mind 37
11. Learning from afflictive emotions 48
12. The gift of forgiveness 54
13. Freedom from stress 58
14. The measure of greatness 61
15. Reality before it happens 64
16. Karma: the gift of free tuition 67
17. Surrendering to love 75
18. Knowledge and compassion 78
19. Emerging vision: parts of the whole 83
20. Magnetic alignment 85
21. Why have a big vision? 99
22. Vision, planning and affirmation exercises 104
23. You and I make the difference 106
24. Summary of Part 1: Purpose and Vision 108

25. A gift received and offered 110
26. Guidelines for Exercises 111
27. Exercise for Chapter 3: Purpose… 113
Life Change 1. Finding my purpose 113
28. Exercises for Chapter 6: Intuition… 120
29. Exercises for Chapter 8: Free will… 123
30. Exercises for Chapter 9: Radiating love 129
Life Change 2. Communicating with the heart 129
31. Exercises for Chapter 11: Learning 130
32. Exercises for Chapter 12: Forgiveness 132
Life Change 3. Forgiveness spring-clean 138
33. Exercises for Chapter 16: Karma 144
34. Exercises for Chapter 17: Love 147
35. Exercises for Chapter 18: Compassion 149
36. Exercises for Chapter 21: Vision 151
I. Notes on My Journey 165
II. Seven Days in Japan 172
III. Personal Diet Practices 194
IV. Index to Part 1: Purpose and Vision 196

IV. The journey to this book

In early 2000, having recently completed a book on business performance management, I was relaxing on an aeroplane from London to Brussels. Then and over the months that followed, much of the core content of this book seemed to dictate itself to me.

The exercises are added, either based on exercises I have experienced in workshops or processes that have unfolded in my life. The personal experiences sections are included at the suggestion of an early reviewer.

V. Science, intent and consciousness

This section provides a few key examples and references that suggest science might be used to explain, or at least understand, the spiritual content of this book. You may choose to skip this section or explore it further by visiting www.MindOfMany.com.

In "Wholeness and the Implicate Order", David Bohm describes an alternative holistic view of the world. This holistic view highlights the assumptions of the mechanistic view that shapes and limits the thoughts we are able to think. "Wholeness and the Implicate Order" is not a new book, or an easy book to read, but it is wonderful and brilliant. Since I read it in the early 80s, it has certainly helped my mind to understand many things that I intuitively know.

In her book, "The Field", Lynn McTaggart provides an easy-to- understand review of science and experiments on topics from prayer and homeopathy to remote viewing, intention and telepathy. "The Field" provides extensive evidence to answer key questions like: "Does prayer and intention impact events?" It explores the evidence for a field of connectedness, a fabric of consciousness.

In "The Field", I was struck by references to experiments relating to Random Event Generators or REGs.

Part I: Purpose and Vision

These devices are completely random. Whatever they do at this moment should not impact what they do in the next moment. They are like perfectly balanced coins being thrown again and again – heads or tails.

Random Event Generators work by the fundamental unpredictability or uncertainty of matter.

To make the point that intention works, consider the following experiment. A group of day-old chicks have been imprinted on a REG. That is they think that the REG is their mother because it is the first thing they saw when they hatched. The REG is set up so that it randomly moves one way or the other depending on its random event generator. The chicks are behind a mesh, but they can see the REG.

When the chicks see the REG, they think it is their mother, so they naturally want it to come towards them. ("Mummy, Mummy, come here!") The surprising result is that the REG spends more time near the chicks than it should according to 'pure chance'.

According to a web abstract from the experimenter René Peoc'h, in another experiment where the REG was carrying a candle with light for the chicks in a dark room. They tested 80 groups of 15 chicks. In 71% of cases the robot spent excessive time in the vicinity of the chicks. In the absence of the chicks, the robot moved randomly. The overall results were statistically significant at $p < 0.01$. That is 1 in 100 chance that they would happen by chance.

Another similar experiment was done with baby rabbits. This time, they could see a REG with a scary flashing red light on the top. They were naturally afraid and wanted it to go away. The surprising result is that the REG did just that and spent time further away from the rabbits than expected according to probability.

The lesson from these experiments and the suggestion from this book is that if a group of baby chicks or rabbits can change the world through intention, so can we.

Another series of experiments shows that intention affects living and non-living systems. In three separate experiments by Dr William Tiller, a group of advanced meditators were given a specific goal to focus on while performing an advanced meditation practice. Experiments focused on three separate goals to affect:
1. pH or acidity of a sample of water;
2. rate of development of fruit fly larvae; and
3. rate of working of a liver enzyme.

In all three cases, under controlled conditions, the intended for result was achieved showing a statistically significant impact of the meditators' intention. There is more to this experiment than explained here. See the paper referenced on www.MindOfMany.com for details.

Dr Tiller suggests that the meditators, through their advanced meditation practice, change the physical "gauge state" (or the rules by which science works) from the ordinary state, where our intention has no impact, to an extraordinary state, where our intention shapes reality.

The lesson I drew from these experiments and from speaking with one of the experimenters is that our intentions can shape reality and our state of mind affects our ability to shape reality.

The Global Consciousness Project is a global experiment consisting of a network of REGs around the world referred to as "Eggs". Each consists of a hardware REG attached to a computer running custom software. The map below is taken from the Global Consciousness Project website.

Part 1: Purpose and Vision

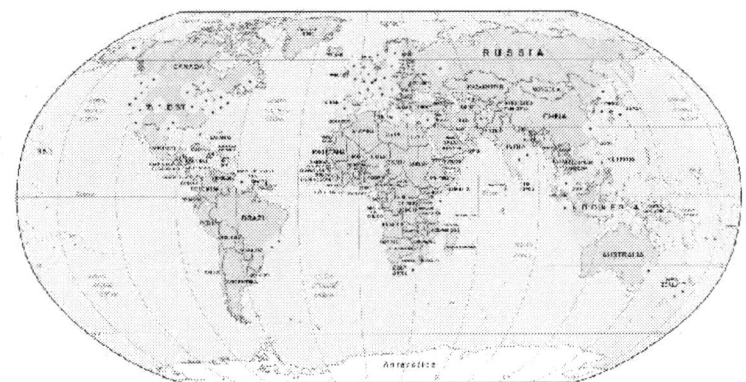

Figure 1: Global Consciousness Project sites

On September 11th 2001, when the attention of many in the world was on the events in New York, the Eggs around the world showed uncharacteristic behaviour. I have chosen one of many statistical graphs from an article on the subject by the Global Consciousness Project Director, Roger Nelson, from the project website. It shows the degree of correlation (relatedness) of the Eggs for September 11th compared to the 60 surrounding days. The results for most of the days shown are expected within a 5% probability.

The September 11th data for up to about 2 hours following the attacks shows a 1 in 2,000 probability. For that period the behaviour of the REGs or "Eggs" ceased to be random!

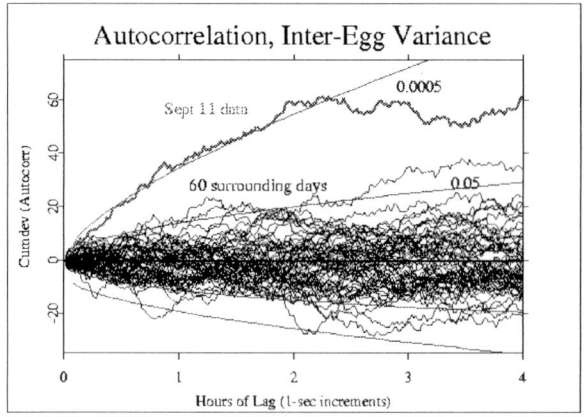

Figure 2: September 11th results from Global Consciousness Project

According to Roger Nelson, Director, Global Consciousness Project in the web article: September 11th 2001: Exploratory and Contextual Analyses

"One way to think of these startling correlations is to accept the possibility that the instruments have captured the reaction of a global consciousness beginning to form. The network was built to do just that: to see whether we could gather evidence of a communal, shared mind in which we are participants even if we don't know it."

The above map, autocorrelation chart and quotation are Copyright © by Roger Nelson for the Global Consciousness Project. All rights reserved.

The above references and experimental examples are given to help our scientific minds to explore the vision and possibility of this book. You and I are not passive observers, but co-creators of

Part I: Purpose and Vision

global consciousness. Who we are, how we behave, what we think, is shaping global consciousness and so shaping our world.

In a world where there is still poverty, injustice, environmental damage, war and terrorism, the necessary and inevitable emerging global transformation depends on us. Its outcome depends on how we play our part.

The part we play depends on who we perceive ourselves to be and on the power that we believe we have.

For links and references, visit WWW.MindOfMany.COM

VI. September 11th 2001: a changing world

For those of us in the rich developed nations, the world has changed. To fulfil our dreams we have to face new challenges. To create and live in this changed world, we must transform ourselves. As we transform ourselves, then our families, our organisations and our institutions will follow.

Before September 11th, when problems stayed localised within sealed borders, wars could be fought in faraway places.

Before September 11th 2001 many of us in the 'developed world' lived safe and secure in a world of certainty. Real danger was something that existed beyond our borders. We were separated by distance from any people who might wish to harm us, separated from danger, mass suffering and war. Somewhere in the world the harvest succeeded and we had the wealth to live – we trusted our economy to provide through boom and recession.

In a world of global communication, media and mass-airtravel, there is no such thing as a faraway place. **After September 11th 2001**, the only guarantee of safety from human threat is to have no enemies. The only guarantee of safety for our financial, governmental and economic systems is that everyone wins when our economic systems succeed. It is not enough that our actions are Fair and Just, they must also be seen to be Fair and Just.

**One person's justice is another person's crime.
To ensure safety and success, we must be understood.
To ensure that we are understood, we must understand.
To understand we must have compassion.**

Today, we are being forced by economic and social necessity to learn and live compassion. Now, questions that lay deep in our collective mind, are brought to the fore:
- What is the point?
- What is *my* purpose?
- How can I have peace of mind?
- How can I make a difference?
- How can we build a better world?

There is a silver lining in the previously unthinkable events of September 11th. We are reminded that we share one planet. Humanity is one family and whenever one of us suffers, we all suffer. Whenever one of us is unsafe, we are all unsafe.

Thoughts about global justice and environmental stewardship used to seem like a luxury. We had to protect our economy above all else, because, like nature for primitive peoples, the economy was our ultimate provider. Now, it is clear that our economy is vulnerable to the actions of people far beyond our borders.

Now, individually and as nations, we are becoming aware that securing our safety demands that we find shared vision and eliminate injustice and suffering in the world. In this New World, Purpose, Forgiveness, Compassion and Love are the currency of success.

Material strength, in money and power, enables success and is secured by success, but material strength alone is not enough.

Material strength gives us no certainty in uncertain times. To find inner strength, we must uncover the power of our human soul by meeting the needs of our human heart.

Purpose, Forgiveness, Compassion and Love are the timeless needs of the human heart, the timeless expressions of the human soul. By coming to know Purpose, Forgiveness, Compassion and Love we come to know the boundless strength of inner certainty.

Through material success, we can develop the means to effect change in the world.

In striving for material strength alone, we have forgotten our spiritual needs. When we forget our spiritual needs, we forgo our own spiritual strength.

We feel uncertain in our world and we build defences and barriers to combat our own fear. When we forget our spiritual needs, no amount of money, laws, policing, munitions and armies will ever be enough to protect us from our own fears.

Until we meet our spiritual needs, we are not whole. Success is hollow.

We can choose to strive for soul strength, by meeting our spiritual needs. When we meet our spiritual needs, we discover our spiritual strength. We experience inner certainty. We experience connectedness with other people, humanity and our planet. We become driven by an authentic desire to develop shared vision and eliminate suffering in the world.

In striving to meet spiritual needs alone, we can forget the material needs of what we spiritually desire. When we forget our material needs, we forgo our material strength. We may feel powerless in our world and retreat into our dreams, rather than face our failure to make those dreams real.

Until we meet our own material needs and the material needs of our dreams, we are not whole. We are impotent and our dreams are hollow.

When we balance material and spiritual needs, we can make our dreams into reality. We can fulfil our soul's desire to build a better world. When we can dream and make our dreams real, we have found wholeness as a human being.

This book offers a path of discovery on our journey to inner strength.

VII. How to use this book

Use the book alone, with a friend or with a group of friends. Compare notes and have fun.

Unless you are drawn to a particular exercise, you may like to read the book first and come back to the exercises that you choose later. People have used the exercises sequentially as a personal development programme. People have also described using the book by opening it at a page randomly to find an insight. Please do what feels right for you. See Guidelines for Exercises on page 111.

See references on www.MindOfMany.com.

So, now let us begin…

Part 1: Purpose and Vision

1. A time of change

Every change creates opportunity: the bigger the change, the bigger the opportunity. Today change is everywhere. A huge wave is gathering, a wave of transformation to sweep across every level of our lives.

We can ride this wave to create a New World or let the wave break around us throwing our lives into turmoil.

To find peace of mind and happiness at this extraordinary gateway moment, we must make our lives extraordinary.

Change works with both the 'stick' of pain that pushes us and the 'carrot' of a vision that gives us courage and pulls us forward.

This vision is a pattern that stretches across humanity. We each see a part of it in our most daring dreams.

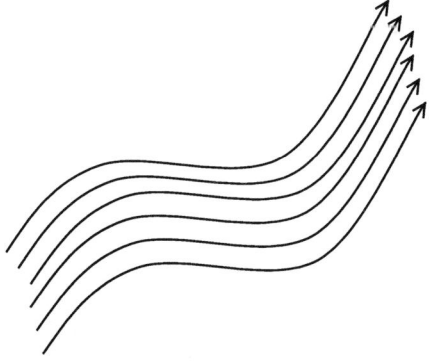

Figure 3: The pattern of the Emerging Global Transformation

If it were one of us alone, feeling the pressure of stress and the pull of vision, then it might be resistible.

Just as the sea cannot help but follow the rising tide, so we are all irresistibly carried by the rising tide of transformation.

In times gone by, people of great vision and courage felt the pull of transformation and saw the possibility of a New World. They played out their lives in pursuit of their dreams. Today, if we dare to change, we have the opportunity to fulfil those dreams.

Do we dare to enter on a journey of transformation that can change our lives and the world for our children?

The question is when pain or vision will give us the courage to change and give up the Old World to take on the challenges of the new. The New World is happening through us:

You and I make the difference.

We most deeply want to develop, grow and transform. The pull of our vision and the pressure from our stress just support us in doing what we want to do anyway.

"What a great time to be alive!"

Personal Experience: Around the middle of 1999, it became obvious that if I continued to do what I had done for the last 15 years, nothing much was likely to change. I'd tried hard work and smart thinking. It didn't seem to work for me. There seemed to be a gap between what I was feeling might be possible and the life that I was living. That was the 'stick' of pain. I began to reach out intuitively, using some of the approaches described later in this book, to try to understand what was going on in the world. What revealed itself to me was an extraordinary and inspiring pattern that has changed my understanding of our world. This is the 'carrot' of vision.

Today, I seem to continually meet people who are at the point of questioning their role and purpose, for example, people who have:
- been caused to reconsider their life direction after losing their work or relationship;
- decided to leave a job or relationship that had satisfied them for years before;
- begun to feel that their work is no longer worthwhile;
- been drawn to do something different, but they are not clear what.

I've found that it can help to suggest that our stress and vision can be a gift, to force us to pay attention to our purpose, forcing us to understand our role in the change that is happening in our world.

In my work with people from organisations and governments and as a citizen, I experience the same dynamic. In the developed world, our governments are pulled by a vision of better service and pushed by complaints about failure of the services we have.

The developed world is pulled to invest in the United Nations and in development by the 'carrot' of vision and now, since September 11th in particular, the 'stick' of fear pushes us – fear of the consequences of disparity and suffering in the world.

Ten years on from the appointment of Nelson Mandela as President, South Africa is pulled by the vision of decent housing for all of its citizens and pushed by the need to deliver on the goal of building new houses as a part of resolving the causes of crime. The same two forces seem to play on people, organisations and societies wherever I look.

Vision on its own is a kind of torture – seeing the future, but not being able to build it. We can either hide from our vision, or change ourselves and join with others so that we can build our vision.

2. The Emerging Global Transformation

As human beings, we use our understanding of things to understand ourselves.

The problem is that the way we think about ourselves limits what we think is possible.

If a bird believed it could not fly, it might never try. The 'Old Science'– with Newton's laws of mechanics – taught us to think of ourselves as separate things, interacting like the famous Newton's Cradle or like billiard balls on a table.

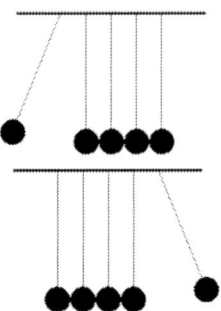

Figure 4: Billiard Ball Reality - Reacting to Circumstances

Part 1: Purpose and Vision

Newton's Cradle: the left-hand ball is pulled back and released. When the left-hand ball strikes the second ball, the ball at the right-hand end is pushed out in reaction.

Newton's Cradle and references on
WWW.MindOfMany.COM

A billiard ball moves automatically, mechanically, without choice, when it is struck by another ball or by the cue. That doesn't mean that we have to react automatically without choice whenever we are struck by external circumstances.

The billiard ball view sees the world as one big machine – science, economics and relationships are just part of the machine. The New Science has moved beyond that. People are not machines, nor are organisations, nor is the weather. The ideas of the Old Science are not sufficient to allow us to meet today's challenges.

The Emerging Global Transformation cannot be understood or described by thinking about billiard balls.

> **Business Experience (South Africa)**
> In January 2001, I was chairing a conference on government performance management in South Africa. One presenter, Kisa Dlamini, Director of Durban Metropolitan Management Services, explained how they are reorganising the city to work consistent with "Batho Pele" or People First – the South African Government initiative to make the needs of people into the driver of government policy and activity. He defined Performance Management as "about managing all the actions taken by members of the organisation to ensure that these actions take the organization closer to its goal".

As suggested later in this book, "Wherever we see systems and structures for improvement and learning, the Emerging Global Transformation is at work". Performance Management is the improvement and learning system of an organisation. The growing importance of Performance Management is one of the many aspects of the Emerging Global Transformation.

The conference showed other examples of this movement of change.

Kisa Dlamini's presentation included the following text, describing the old, fragmented way of thinking and the new, holistic, way of thinking and how they apply to organisations and performance management.

"Ways of Thinking or Assumptions
At the base of it all are assumptions or ways of thinking. An assumption is a worldview or how [we think] things work in life. A way of thinking is the foundation of all policies, measurements, rewards, training and the explanation of behaviour in [an] organisation.

There are basically two ways of thinking, namely the activity-based and fragmented (parts) thinking [and] results-based and holistic thinking.

Fragmented & Activity Based Thinking
It assumes that the reality is made up of a number of isolated parts that are static.

The whole is the sum total of its parts - if one gets the isolated parts right, the whole will come right.

Process is a group of unconnected activities. The best way of understanding it is to list the activities and deal with each independently.

Holistic and results based thinking
Reality is made up of a number of interdependent parts that are in a constant state of change and development, a change in one leads to a change in another.

The whole is more than the sum total of its parts - one can only understand the part within the context of the whole.

Process is a series of interdependent events that deliver a result or output. The best way of understanding it is to start with the result and the process that delivers it."

The presentation was extremely insightful and included case studies of dramatic service improvements resulting from applying these ideas. When I asked, Kisa Dlamini said Peter Senge was the key influencer to his thinking in this area.

If the Emerging Global Transformation cannot be understood by thinking about billiard balls, or by thinking about parts alone, is there science that can help us to understand how this New World is emerging? Welcome to the New Sciences: of uncertainty, 'chaos theory', of self-organising systems, of fractals. Einstein opened the door to a New World where things and energy are the same. Heisenberg (with the 'Uncertainty Principle') made it clear that we affect whatever we see. Our perception, what we think and how we feel about it, make a difference. But as individuals, in organisations and as society, we wait by the threshold of the New World, not daring to cross and apply this New Science. Why?

Because the implications are terrifying – everything we do makes a difference – everything!

Not just our actions, but also our thoughts and perceptions, make a difference. How we think about things shapes the future. We create the future, through our perception. We own the future.

If we own the future, there's no one else to blame. If we own the future, then how we think and what we do about it defines the world for our children.

Our thoughts and actions define the world for our children.

When we thought that the world was a billiard-ball machine, the most we could do was to kick back. Even leaders were powerless, they had to keep driving and fuelling and servicing their part of the machine. No wonder our leaders suffer from every kind of stress – they had all the responsibility and still no choice, because, after all, it was just a machine.

In the world where we own the future, anything is possible. The New Science of Chaos Theory says that a butterfly flapping its wings in China can result in a storm in North America and if that weren't true, computers could predict the weather – and they can't! The draught from a tiny butterfly wing can change a weather system. Tiny actions can give rise to huge consequences. This is a key point, so spend a moment to consider what it might mean about the difference that you and I can make with our seemingly tiny actions.

The New Science of Chaos Theory says that something very small can give rise to something very big. A butterfly wing flapping in China can result in a storm in the USA.

Intuitively we know this, but it is only recently that our popular understanding of science has confirmed it. Chaos Theory has huge implications for the way that we think about and understand our world.

MindOfMany.COM has links and books on New Science.

So, it was safe in the Old World because the difference we could make as individuals was limited by our individual resources and capabilities, or to use an analogy, by the size of our butterfly wings.

In the New World, one flap of the wing is enough. Size doesn't matter!

Changing the world starts with you and me through our tiniest actions. No excuses. And the good news is – anything is possible.

Quite a responsibility! It could feel like a burden, but there is more good news. The New Science says that we don't need so much to make things happen as to 'happen them'. Things emerge. The future is emerging. A global transformation is underway – in our lives, in organisations, in government, in politics, in technology and in society. These transformations don't just fit together because someone designed them that way; they fit together because they are aspects of the same emerging world.

Everything we see fits together because it is all a part of the Emerging Global Transformation.

So, where do you and I fit in? There is more awesome responsibility and opportunity. Everything that has happened in our life journey: every event, coincidence, contact, skill, relationship, capability brings you and me to this moment now. And now we have a choice in every moment and our choices make a difference. Does the butterfly flap its wing to the left, resulting in typhoons across the southeast USA or to the right, resulting in bumper harvests across a previously drought-stricken continent? Our choices, even the seemingly small ones, can make a difference. Perhaps you and I do not just make a difference; perhaps you and I make *the* difference!

**We really understand the opportunity of the Emerging Global Transformation when we recognise for ourselves that:
"*I* make the difference".**

So, holding your life in your hands, mastering every atom of destiny that you have ever experienced: how will you make the future, which you own? What world will you leave for our children?

At some points in time, the butterfly wing may make no difference – it is lost in the global weather pattern. Now is not that time.

Now is a time when the destiny of humanity and our planet are being determined for hundreds of years, if not for millennia to come.

On the one hand, we are painfully aware of the vulnerability of all of us to the acts of others creating uncertainty and the potential for fear. We have no choice but to embrace and understand the needs of other peoples, religions, societies and nations. On the other hand, we sense new connections, new opportunities. There is a shift in the way we think. This shift accelerated with the new millennium and all that we made it mean and with the surge of activity in the "New Economy" of ideas, communities and technology. The dotcom boom and dotcom bust has left its legacy. The new communications technology and the web allow us to extend our network of influence and share our purpose, our vision and our projects with millions of people across the planet. We can learn from one another, create a shared vision and collaborate to make it happen. What new ways of thinking and working can we adopt so as to emerge a shared vision across a community, and across our planet?

You and I own the future, so now when every stroke of our butterfly wings makes a difference, now when every action we take makes a difference, what will we choose? If the future is emerging and if you and I make the difference, how do we make the right choices and flap our wings in the correct direction?

What can we trust to steer by in this world where tiny actions can produce immense outcomes?

3. The true joy in life: serving a purpose

There is nothing so inevitable as an idea whose time has come. In a time where we search for meaning, the time has come for knowing and living by purpose.

There is nothing on earth so powerful as a human being aligned with purpose.

Purpose is personal, but it is also impersonal. As we align with our own deepest purpose, we align with the Emerging Global Transformation.

To play our part in the Emerging Global Transformation, we can make two simple but life-changing choices:

1. Choose to know and steer by my Purpose.
   Purpose is our reason for being, our guiding light and inner direction.
2. Choose to develop and follow my Intuition. Intuition is the only way to choose between flapping the butterfly wing to the left or to the right. ***Intuition is our inner tuition – our contact***

with the will of the unfolding, Emerging Global Transformation. When we follow our intuition we can play our part in unfolding a future worth choosing.

In a moment, intuition can give us an understanding that might otherwise take hours for the mind to unravel and explain, just as in a moment a picture can reveal what could take hours to describe. Now we can make the two choices...

I choose to know and steer by my purpose.
I choose to develop and follow my intuition.
The world will never be the same again.

These are two simple choices, but making them, committing to them is a destiny-changing act – like taking a marriage vow, or promising obedience to a spiritual discipline.

If we are to keep these promises, they must form the basis of our new thinking and change our habits and behaviour.

To quote George Bernard Shaw:

"For this is the true joy in life. To be used by a purpose recognised by yourself as a mighty one. Life is no brief candle to me; it is a kind of splendid torch, which we have for the moment before passing to future generations. I want to be thoroughly used up when I die".

There is no greater purpose than unfolding the future of our most daring dreams. Yet it is hard to commit to this new unknown master. How can we dare and prepare to make this commitment? We will never know the bliss, comfort and certainty of serving a mighty purpose until we have dared to commit to it. Can I look into my soul and see my purpose without first having to throw away who I know myself to be? Yes. Can I learn to follow the light of my intuition without having to give up on my intellect? Yes.

The following pages provide a simple exercise to reveal your purpose and release the courage to follow it and to choose and own our future.

To know who you are, know your purpose.
To experience satisfaction, fulfil your purpose.
To experience joy, live your purpose.
To inspire someone, let them see their purpose.
To know someone, know their purpose.
To serve someone, serve their purpose.
To create partnership, align on purpose.
To create a new world – teach people to teach people to live by purpose.

The short step and profound transformation to living from purpose, guided by intuition, can be scary. To uncover the crystal clarity of our purpose, we must, for a moment, distract our minds. Then we can introduce our mind to its rightful master - purpose.

34% of people said that the one question they would ask a Supreme Being if they could get a direct and immediate answer would be *"What is my purpose here?"*

USA Today, from a survey for the Lutheran Brotherhood.

Confirming or finding or refining your purpose does not need to be difficult.

Choosing to know and steer by my purpose

Since not all of us find it easy to get direct answers from a Supreme Being, the "Purpose Life Change" is very helpful.

Personal Experience: I have used the Purpose Life Change myself several times. When I used it, most recently in spring 2005, I gained profound, life changing insights. From my personal experience, I recommend this exercise.

I have also facilitated the exercise with many people, sometimes with a single person, sometimes with groups of hundreds. I have had great feedback from people who have done it on their own using this book. It works. Some of my most fruitful relationships have developed rapidly because we recognised that we had aligned purpose.

One hour spent with this exercise could change your life forever. You may choose to spend twenty minutes or a few days working with the exercise to explore your purpose more deeply. If you don't want to do it now as an exercise, you can skip the following shaded pages. Why spend another day without revealing or confirming the clear guiding light of purpose?

You will need a pen and paper and Purpose Life Change: **Finding my purpose on page 113.** Write notes as you do the exercise.

4. Vision: the tidal pull of Global Transformation

Personal Experience: I remember that when my life was not working, when I was not proud of what I had accomplished, I did not want to create a vision, I guess because it would have made me even more aware of my sense of failure in what I had achieved so far. I waited to achieve more before I developed my vision. When I finally dared to develop, or even acknowledge, a vision, it seemed to become a magnet for the circumstances of my life. When we took time out to develop a vision for our business, it was very painful for some of the people on the team. They couldn't see the point, when we had more basic issues. They thought that we did not need more vision. We needed more results. For me, this clarified that we have to work on both vision and results. As a person, I need to have a vision *and* take the steps to make it real. As a person, I need the support of a relationship and structures (like home) in place and the disciplines (in work, exercise, diet) to be able to deliver my vision. A business is the same, it needs a vision and a strategy and plan and it needs customers, facilities, IT structures and processes to be able to deliver its vision. I have encouraged and coached other people in developing vision. It does take courage, but it can transform circumstances. The same struggle has meaning and purpose when we are working towards a vision. Without vision, we may fail to recognise the opportunities which life is offering us all the time. (As researched by Dr. Richard Wiseman and reported in his book The Luck Factor, lucky people create and recognise opportunity.)

Knowing our purpose is uplifting, but to experience profound and sustained satisfaction, we must live our purpose and start to leave its

impact in our community and on the world. Our vision is the blueprint for this impact.

We all have the gift of vision, but we may not have the habits and practices that allow us to access that gift. Vision is our ability to create a future in our minds. Our opportunity is to create a vision that gives expression to our purpose, rather than being only based on and limited by our past. To become masters of vision, we must learn to leave the sufferings of the past behind us as we create and explore possibility.

Once we have seen the vision of a future worth choosing, it pulls us forward, to find the people, resources and partnerships to make it real.

Through today's technology we have unlimited ability to communicate, network and partner. We can share and utilise the resources of others so the limits are defined not by our own resources, but by our ability to create win-win partnerships. Our purpose sets us free by showing us who we are. Our vision shows us what can be and what to make of our lives and our world. Through our own highest vision, we catch glimpses of the blueprint of the Emerging Global Transformation.

All the changes in our lives, businesses, societies, governments, the New Economy and the Internet, are facets of the Emerging Global Transformation.

In a challenging and sometimes stressful world, how can we stay on purpose and play our part in the Emerging Global Transformation?

5. The Zen Archer: aligning with purpose

"The Zen Archer waits with bow and arrow poised and releases the arrow. The arrow hits the target. She prepares to release another arrow, releases it and the arrow misses the target. She breathes deeply again, quietens her mind, then releases another arrow that finds its way to the centre of the target."

According to ancient texts that became the bible, to sin was to fire the arrow of life in such a way as to miss the target. Repentance is to understand that you are off track, or not pointing at the target, in such a way that you naturally correct your misalignment with the target.

Our life is on target when our living, thoughts and actions are lined up with our purpose. Joy is the natural outcome of having the arrow aligned with the target.

To sin is simply to release the arrow without stilling the mind, without aligning with purpose. The outcome is that the arrow misses the target. Suffering suggests that we need to realign with our purpose (repent) so that the arrow of our life naturally meets the target (providing the satisfaction of fulfilling our purpose) in the future.

Personal Experience: I was given the example of the Zen Archer to explain sin and repentance by the late physicist David Bohm in the early 1980s. My Japanese translator in 2002, Kawano san, told me that the kanji character for Purpose in Japanese is made up of two kanji characters, one meaning 'aim for' or 'see', the other meaning 'target'.

The Zen Archer	Our Lives
Release arrow	Take action
Quiet mind	We'll talk about that later.
Miss target, or 'off the mark'	Action is off purpose
Hit target, or 'on the mark'.	Action is on purpose

Biblical Language	Our Lives
Sin	Acting without aligning with purpose. Being 'off the mark'.
Repentance	Noticing that we are off purpose in such a way that we get back on purpose. Getting back 'on the mark'.

What do we do when we miss the target? Correct our alignment with purpose? We'll talk about how later.

- When we experience profound joy – we are probably aligned with purpose.
- When we experience mental or emotional suffering – we are probably not aligned with purpose.

How can I make sure that I use this learning? Promise myself, my family, my friends, a Supreme Being and the Universe, that whenever I am off purpose, I will immediately correct my misalignment.

The necessity of a 'still mind'

To get back on the mark, the Zen Archer had to still her mind.

Without a still mind, I cannot dependably get on purpose or stay on purpose.

6. Intuition: the gift of personal guidance

Personal Experience: My first memory of intuition was when, as a five year old, I was told by a nun, Sister Ignatius, that I would likely go to hell if I did not believe in God. This did not feel right and I concluded that if there was a God, then God would see inside my heart and motivations and realise that I was not that bad, so I would be fine. Years later, I feel pretty much the same way. I have a deep, abiding sense of a benevolent Universal power.

Some things are not to be proven but can only be felt, intuited, known. Let us use the story of the Zen Archer to understand how we can access intuition. How did the Zen Archer know which way to point the arrow to get back on the mark? She followed her intuition – her *inner tuition*.

To come to know the simple pervasive peace of being steered by intuition, we must ask for and listen to new inputs.

Intuition = Inner Tuition

Intuition, inner guide or inner tuition

In one of those paradoxes of scale that turn up in modern science and ancient mysticism, when we listen deep inside for inner tuition, we hear the song of the Emerging Global Transformation and gain insight into the working of the Universe around us.

Our purpose provides the ingredients, the raw material, which we are to contribute to building a New World, or as we refer to it earlier, a Future Worth Choosing. Free will – acting from peace and serenity, rather than reacting from afflictive emotions of anger, guilt, upset and fear - allows us to make choices. Intuition is how we see, hear and feel the unfolding pattern of the Emerging Global Transformation, so that we naturally know which choices to make to play our part.

If our life's journey is to grow in quality of character, to grow spiritually, by crossing a mountain range, then our intuition is there to guide us gently to the quiet mountain passes that make the crossing easier.

We must cross the rugged mountains to fulfil our unique and personal spiritual quest and to play our part in the Emerging Global Transformation. Without our intuition, we must still cross the mountain range, but we may scale perilous cliffs and clamber across freezing windswept mountaintops.

Spiritual growth is about developing our quality of character. It is about becoming who we can become and contributing all that we have brought to contribute. The journey can be hard or easy. Our intuition helps to make it easy.

Our spiritual quest is to cross the mountain range. It is our choice how we cross it.

When the going gets tough, it is time to get smarter.

If we want joy, we live from our purpose.

And if we want to find a way forward, we look to our intuition to show the next step.

My intuition shows me the way forward.

Many of us have trained our minds to think, analyse and reason, but we may only think and reason within the bounds of what is reasonable, what fits with the past and with our mental debris or fears.

My intuition gives me access to the unthinkable.

You may have seen "magic eye" pictures that look at first like a meaningless sea of tiny patterns. The harder and more intensely we look and analyse, the more we see the disorder. Only when we relax our focus can the symphony of pattern break through, projecting an image into three dimensions.

Suddenly, in a moment of revelation the third dimension appears. Now a larger pattern emerges, giving depth to the un-discerned folds and wrinkles within the pattern, which moments ago seemed to be random. Just because sometimes we have not seen the three-dimensional image within the totality, that doesn't mean there isn't one. Just because someone else can see it, and they tell us it is beautiful, that doesn't mean they can make us see it.

Our intuition is the soft relaxed focus, which allows us to see the pattern of the Universe. The pattern is the Emerging Global Transformation and each of us has our part to play. The pattern is there and it is awesome, beautiful and never so strong as today.

As we cross the mountains of our spiritual development, our intuition can lead us towards places that we may fear.

If our intuition leads us to a high mountain pass avoiding the ravages of a mountain peak, we must be masters of our fears, responsible for them, not controlled by them, so that we may pass safely and correctly and reach our destined future.

Nurturing Intuition

So, with the resource of our purpose, how do we develop the guiding light of intuition? How do we learn to see the awesome, beautiful pattern of the Emerging Global Transformation and to understand our part in it?
Silence is the key.
Inner truth comes with silence.

If we can learn to empty our minds of the thoughts that normally crowd them and, for example, ask a simple question, the pictures or thoughts that come are guides towards an answer.

The message may require our mind to germinate it, our intellect to strengthen it, but our goal is to have our intuition provide the seed.

Personal Experience: At times in my life, I became almost completely unaware of my intuitive ability, because I did not take the necessary steps to develop and use it. I got into a rut of working harder to try to solve problems, rather than stepping back and using intuition. I spent many years in school and university training my mind. Looking back, the times when I was successful were the times when I was able to apply my intuition as well as my intellect. My own intuition works better when I am 'in good shape', in terms of mental stillness, exercise, feeling well. For years, there was no quiet in my life. I would work long and hard, then come home and turn on the television. No wonder life was tough! I now make a priority of nurturing my intuition. The exercises in this book reflect what I have found works in nurturing my own intuition. In the past, my weighting of working, intellect and using intuition was in favour of hard work, followed by intellect, followed by intuition.

> I now seek to have my intuition guide my intellect and to have my intellect guide my actions and my work.

If you have spent years in formal education, what level of attention might you now be prepared to apply to the following:
- Exploring your intuitive ability?
- Developing intuitive ability?
- Using your intuitive ability?

The more we learn to know and trust our intuition, the easier and more fertile this source of information becomes.

To work with our intuition, these four guideline steps work: -
1. Stilling the mind
2. Becoming receptive, or asking questions
3. Listening, understanding
4. Acting on the answers

The first step towards intuition is stilling the mind, the subject of the next section.

> **Personal Experience**: In early 2001, I had an extraordinary, synchronicity-filled business trip to Japan. I felt compelled to write a diary the morning after I returned. I've included that diary as "Appendix II: Seven Days in Japan".
> It is an example of how I've experienced being guided and directed to see patterns and learn intuitively. For example the trip revealed to me a deeper understanding of the role of the quality movement in business and governments, the gift of Hiroshima to the world and connections between Buddhism and Christianity.

23

7. Stillness: the gift of peace of mind

Fear, anger, old resentments, coffee, junk food and stimulants can all get in the way of mental silence. It is hard to have a still mind when our body is filled with stress.

There are many relaxation and meditation techniques. A still mind can be enhanced by the relaxation of sleep, or in the receptive serenity that follows the intense activity of sustained physical exercise. Nature is calming. We can find peace of mind by walking in nature, for example by being close to healthy plants and healthy lakes, rivers and fountains. Since our body is, at many levels, a reflection of our mind, stretching, yoga, martial arts and massage can all help to still the mind. Giving and receiving emotional and physical tenderness is also relaxing.

Personal Experience: So long as I take good care of myself, in terms of body care and home/work balance, the same stilling of my mind, through meditation or sleep seems to provide different information depending on my needs. My intuition is more active now. Frequently, I wake up at four in the morning with a clear message in my mind. For a moment I used to wish that the clarity would go away, so that I could go back to sleep. This only lasted moments as I remembered years in 'the wilderness' where I felt like a castaway into a world of relentless struggle, knowing and also doubting that life would some day allow me to express my deepest commitments.

I pick up paper and pen and start to write. Early morning clarity has given almost all of the original text for this book. More recently, the same clarity gave me solutions to other challenges, for example:

- An approach to organising the business processes in a company

- A step-by-step approach to help one of our government customers to begin the process of transformation
- A model for understanding organisational transformation in terms of acupuncture

In the early 80s, I learned Transcendental Meditation. I discovered that I could clear stress or the tired energy from working on a computer. Over the last twenty years, I have experienced different forms of meditation and contemplation.

Personal Experience: The Brahma Kumaris

In 2002, at the World Summit for Sustainable Development in Joburg, I came across the Brahma Kumaris (BKs) and the Living Values programme which connects people with their experience of fundamental human values. Several synchronicities including recommendations from colleagues in Kenya and friends in Geneva led my partner Gina and me to one of their meditation retreats in 2003. Since then, we have found ourselves connecting more and more with the 'BKs' including a magical visit to the headquarters of the "Brahma Kumaris World Spiritual University" or BKWSU at Mount Abu in Rajasthan, India.

I wrote the core of this book about the Emerging Global Transformation in 2000. The BKs have, for over 50 years, recognised the coming of the "Confluence Age", the time of transition between an increasingly chaotic world and a new world of human elevation, collaboration and compassion. As individuals and as an organisation, they demonstrate what this new world might be. The BKs have not only envisioned global transformation, they are supporting people around the world to play their part - providing free meditation classes and retreats from over

6,000 centres. In my experience of the BKs they embody the principle of "Be the change you wish to see".

In Mount Abu I was inspired and moved. There is a pervasive sense of peace. Everything is beautifully and consciously cared for. As guests we were served with both love and respect.

At the bottom of the mountain is a gathering place for 20,000 people. The solar cooking system can cook over 30,000 meals a day. When Gina and I were there for "Peace Of Mind 2004", they were also hosting a conference on "Meditation as Medicine". In the BKWSU headquarters at the top of the mountain, there are rooms dedicated to transformation of the professions, for example Values-based Media, Values-based Jurors and Values-based Politicians.

As an NGO, the BKWSU performed a global survey of vision and human values from which the Living Values programme came.

The BKs teach a meditation method called Raj Yoga. Attending their retreats and centres in the UK, India and Africa has been a great pleasure and a gift in my life and in the lives of several of our friends.

I was amused to find that the 4am time, when most of this book was written, is called in Hindi "Amrit Vela" or "early morning hours of nectar", because it is a time when most people are sleeping so there is stillness and the possibility of sweet meditation.

For BK links, visit WWW.MindOfMany.COM.

In the formal education of the West, we spend years learning to read, do sums, to solve problems, to analyse situations, but we are often given no formal instruction, practices or disciplines for relaxation and stilling the mind.

If we had declared reading to be nonsense when we saw the first strange shapes of letters, or arithmetic to be nonsense when we saw the first jumble of numbers called a sum, think what we might have missed!

To give stilling the mind through meditation a proper chance, try to do it at least once a day for at least a month, preferably at the same time each day. If you want to prove to yourself the value, then choose a goal for your meditation practice – happiness, guidance, tranquillity, reduced pulse rate or blood pressure. For the subjective measures, you could rate yourself each day on a scale of 0-10 depending on how happy, guided or tranquil you feel that day.

There are many techniques to help to still the mind.

A Simple Breath Meditation on page 120. It is a technique that anyone can use.

If you can dedicate twenty minutes to an effective meditation practice morning and evening, the peace of mind and serenity that grows from it, will seep out into and come to pervade your life.

You may like to keep a pen and paper beside you as you meditate, so that as your intuition shows you new insights, you can make a note of them without disturbing your quiet state.

The many practices and disciplines of meditation open a wonderful, rich inner world for exploration. You may already have a preferred meditation that works well for you, or you may like to try the following variations and hopefully find someone who is on the same journey to share your experiences.

Personal Experience: I find a deep level of calm and connection by using something like these exercises regularly. When I am walking or running through the beautiful countryside around our home in Yorkshire I feel that I am being recharged. I sometimes enhance my sense of recharge by using something like these exercises. Over time, perhaps 20 years, I have become able to touch this level of calm more quickly. If I am feeling stressed or agitated, I remember to take a moment to find calm. I might do this during a long breath while shopping or while chairing a meeting or presenting a workshop. It works. I am reminded of the words: "the kingdom of heaven is within us". This is how it feels to me when I connect through stillness or meditation.

For simple, easy-to-use exercises to experiment with meditation, see *Exercise 2. Breath Meditation: sinking deep infinite blackness* on page 121 and *Exercise 3. A Breath Meditation: transmitting and being charged with Universal Power* on page 122.

Kundalini Yoga: Towards the end of 2000, I accidentally attended a Kundalini Yoga class in place of the step aerobics class I had expected. I had done various aerobic exercises for 20 years and various simple yoga exercises on and off for about the same length of time. Even during the initial exercises of the class, I could intuitively feel the Kundalini Yoga working on my chakras (energy centres). Some exercises affect specific meridians or energy lines in the body. Sometimes I can feel the specific meridian (energy line) or chakra activated or tingling during the exercise. At the end of a session, my whole nervous and emotional system is re-energised. Since first discovering this yoga practice, I have frequently used a set of exercises from the Kundalini Yoga website and more recently the beautiful book by my yoga teacher, Siri Data.

Part I: Purpose and Vision

> The website www.MindOfMany.COM has current links for Kundalini Yoga including Siri Data's book and the specific exercise set that I regularly use.

For meditation and yoga links visit WWW.MindOfMany.COM.

These and other meditations can help us to explore our inner world and experience the energies that pervade the vastness of our consciousness.

Through meditation we create the silent mind through which the quiet voice of intuition can be heard.

With passive meditation, we quiet our mind to allow the Emerging Global Transformation to speak to us. Meditation can help to give us freedom from our reactive mind, so that we no longer need to behave like a billiard ball in reaction to external events.

When our reactions are not determined by external events, we can have free will, peace of mind and even bliss.

When anger, guilt, upset, and fear drive our reactions, how do we then reclaim free will?

8. Reclaiming free will

Afflictive Emotions are the emotions of anger, guilt, upset and fear that take away our ability to think clearly and hence our free will. Less obviously, passionate desire or commitment, for example, is also an afflictive emotion because it can also take away our ability to make balanced choices.

Why should plans fail even when they would deliver a win-win for everyone involved? Even when wars are a lose-lose for everyone, why do they still happen?

To serve our purpose, we need to learn to recognise and manage the *afflictive emotions* of anger, guilt, upset, and fear that steal our ability to think clearly.

To free ourselves and the world, we must master our afflictive emotions.

Earlier, we suggested that purpose is the key to experiencing joy and satisfaction. If it were that easy to experience profound feelings of joy and satisfaction, wouldn't everyone be doing it? How come we still suffer? What is the point of the suffering?

> **Personal Experience**: I learned the term afflictive emotion from reading the Dalai Lama's book "Ancient Wisdom, Modern World". Recognising afflictive emotions opened up a world of insight. I now believe that when I make a decision or take an action based on anger, guilt, upset, and fear, or even passion, it is likely to be a mistake. I try to correct these mistakes as quickly as possible. When I am 'in' an afflictive emotion, my ego always believes that the emotion is right and pushes me on, so it is not always easy. I also now recognise afflictive emotions as a potential gift, to show me where I need to learn and grow! I'll leave commenting on that until later.

Let us return to the Zen Archer. To get back on the mark, the Zen Archer quieted her mind and adjusted her aim. The next arrow found its mark. We can ***choose*** to use suffering, the absence of joy, to indicate that we are off the mark – that there is something for us to learn.

Suffering is the absence of joy. When I live my purpose, I return to joy.

When you feel the absence of joy, practise saying: "I am off the mark, so what do I need to do or correct to get back on the mark?"

We can *choose* to use suffering to help us to grow as we return to joy. This does *not* mean that it is true that anyone who suffers needs to grow or that they are to blame. Choosing to see our own suffering this way does not mean that we should not be compassionate to those who suffer.

It is up to other people to consider how they should relate to their suffering, not for us to hold or give an opinion. Better to ask when we see someone else suffering: "How am I off the mark that they are suffering." Rather than: "How are they off the mark that they are suffering?"

In some cultures, our suffering is understood as a result of karma. See Karma: the gift of free tuition on page 67.

Understanding karma is not a tool for judging and correcting others, but a tool for learning and growing ourselves.

Each of us has the opportunity to be responsible for everything that we see and experience. No one can tell us to do it; they can merely point to the opportunity. The more suffering that we choose to become responsible for, the more we expand who we know ourselves to be.

A long time after people first achieved results, created inventions or painted paintings, Newton 'discovered' gravity and his Laws of Mechanics to model how physical things interact. The model was so simple and clear that its assumption and paradigm (or model for thinking) of separated independent objects, interacting through clear physical boundaries, spread way beyond machines and physical objects. It spread into the way we think about everything from social justice to our physical health and emotions. We sought to expand the use of Newton's simply expressed ideas beyond the world of describing billiard balls. By doing this, we strengthened a view of ourselves as objects, our emotional and commercial relationships as interactions – like billiard balls being struck by the cue of life and striking one another.

This paradigm or way of thinking about emotions and humanity robs us of our free will. If we are machines, we don't have choices – we just react. Without free will, we are no longer responsible for the life we live, for our experience of joy. And as billiard balls in the game of life, we are not responsible for the impact we have on other people. In the paradigm where we are billiard balls, billiard balls only move when other billiard balls strike them. The impact they have on others is a result of external causes with no free will or choice. In this paradigm, the buck stops nowhere; the destiny of the world is in no-one's hands. In this paradigm, we only impact others because of what happened to us, not through any choice.

In the billiard ball paradigm, *nobody* has free will and *nobody* makes a difference.

We have scaled the billiard-ball model of reality from our personal relationships to the way we think about social groups and nations. Billiard-ball thinking allows separate nations to react rationally (like billiard balls) and go to war (striking other billiard balls), not necessarily because anyone has a choice in the matter, but because none of us has any choice.

Afflictive emotions of anger, guilt, upset, and fear steal my peace of mind. When I react out of afflictive emotion, I have no free will.

We can reclaim free will by reclaiming our peace of mind. Before we can do this, it is useful to recognise that we are all prey to billiard-ball thinking, where we react to circumstances out of anger, guilt, upset, and fear, rather than choosing our responses.

Choosing how we ACT and REACT

In life we sometimes live from the past. Past pain and upset colour the choice we have in our present, our ability to have peace of mind, live joyfully and create a future worth choosing. If you can remember, or imagine, more carefree times than today then take the opportunity of the following exercises to pause for a moment in the fast pace of life, to renew yourself, by sweeping away the ghosts of the past. The following three simple exercises bring us face to face with potentially life-changing questions.

Transformation lets us evolve to make choices from clear thinking and to live our choices with power.

How can we become aware of and give up our afflictive in favour of more productive emotions?

Try **Exercise 4. I have a choice about REACTING with afflictive emotions** on page 123 and **Exercise 5. I have a choice about ACTING FROM afflictive emotions** on page 124.

In **Exercise 6. Seeing afflictive emotions at work** on page 125, you reflect on the consequences of afflictive emotions.

These exercises provide insight and motivation to 'clean up' the consequences of past afflictive emotions. One powerful way to clean up and complete is through forgiveness. The exercises section of this book includes several forgiveness exercises on page 132.

EFT: A simple tool for dissolving afflictive emotions

Emotional Freedom Technique (EFT) is a powerful and simple tool for dissolving and eliminating afflictive emotion. It is a very simple self-massage, where you tap meridian points of acupuncture, with your finger tips. You tap a sequence of acupuncture points while holding the afflictive emotion in mind. The results are phenomenal. Don't skip this exercise. I highly recommend it. I have used EFT to:

- dissolve stress, anger and upset related to conflict;
- release attachment to a past relationship;
- release inappropriate physical desire.

Exercise 7. on page 126 provides simple steps to try EFT.

MindOfMany.COM has further EFT links.

9. Radiating love

If our goal is to bring love and peace to the world, the heart is a powerful communication tool.

The human body is a vibrating energy system. Whatever we may say through words, we are continually radiating an electromagnetic field.

When we are bathed in afflictive emotions, we radiate disturbed energy and we are likely to experience disturbances in return.

When we are bathed in love, we radiate love and we get back love.

HeartMath: measuring the loving heart

The HeartMath® website describes the HeartMath System as "a set of practical techniques and technologies to help people transmute stress and negative emotions in the moment, improve performance and enrich the quality of life".

Their Freeze-Framer software comes with a finger sensor that plugs into a personal computer. I used it to watch my heart rate vary with time. I experimented with their standard approach to dissolving afflictive emotion and with other approaches I have learned in the past.

I noticed that focusing on and controlling my breath through meditation had an immediate effect on my heart, as did saying the Lords Prayer with reverence and power.

With simple exercises, I learned to intentionally manage the function of my heart from afflictive emotions like anger and frustration to love and appreciation. Having spent a few hours learning the technique by interacting with a software program, I now use it frequently.

The Freeze-Frame tool is easy to learn without the discipline of years of meditation or the requirement of religious belief. I found it so effective and useful, that it would be difficult to forget.

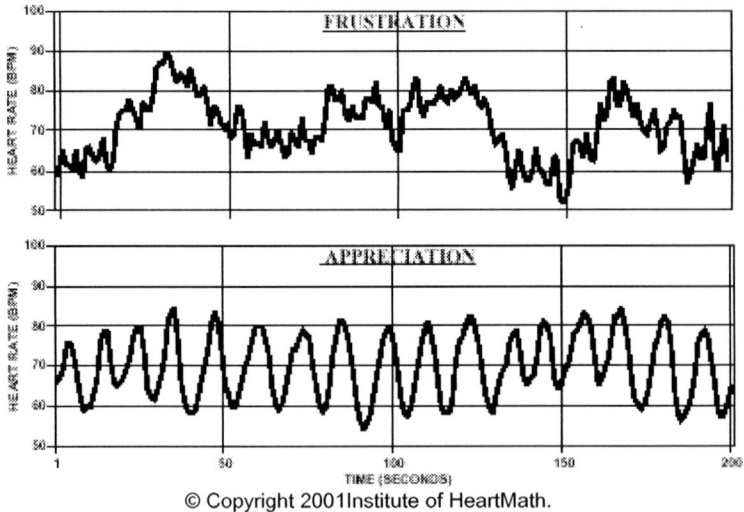

Figure 5: Heart Rate Variability during frustration and appreciation

The graphic above, taken with permission from the HeartMath website, shows heart rate variability – the changing frequency at which the heart beats over time. The random, jerky heart rate variability pattern in the upper graph is typical of afflictive emotions like anger or frustration. The smooth, flowing pattern below is typical of sincere appreciation and love.

I have used the Freeze-Frame technique and Freeze-Framer software to:

- return to centre when I am stressed;
- project love, peace and nurturing to another person;
- create a vibration of love and project it to a baby rabbit to encourage it to bottle-feed;
- understand the physiological symptoms of afflictive emotion;

- understand the role of the heart as the natural governor for the body's rhythms;
- understand the role of the heart as an organ of intuitive thought.

The website for this book has several current links for HeartMath and the Freeze-Frame technique including scientific papers on the effect of afflictive emotions on the heart and HeartMath on afflictive emotions.

Life Change 2. Communicating with the heart on page 129 developed from using the Freeze-Frame technique. It provides a practical exercise to experience and use your heart as a transmitter and communicator of loving energy. If you try this exercise and practise, the results can be wonderful.

MindOfMany.COM has HeartMath and the Freeze-Frame links.

10. The beautiful garden of my mind

Imagine that when we have peace of mind, our mind is like a beautiful garden. The garden is well-maintained and has clear paths and flowerbeds. It has boundary fences to protect it from damage.

The incomplete items identified in the exercises above are like mechanical debris strewn in great pieces across the beautiful garden of our mind. Imagine it like the debris from an aeroplane crash that has destroyed the natural beauty and flattened the fences and boundaries. To enjoy the garden, we need to clean up the garden and repair the fences. Otherwise, we will be forced to spend our lives dodging debris, rather than walking blissfully around paths in the garden. Out of fear, we build fences around the debris, but we leave the garden boundaries un-repaired.

In life, we dodge debris by avoiding difficult or uncomfortable issues out of fear. The debris is anger that we need to release, people to forgive, issues to clean up, guilt to give up, grief and upset to release.

The fences that we build to hide our issues immediately inhibit our movement.

They are the defence mechanisms we use to stop people getting 'close to us', revealing our pain or our anger. The un-repaired garden boundaries are our neglected personal boundaries, which could preserve our self-respect and keep us safe from hurt.

The way that we treat others and allow others to treat us defines our boundaries. It can be hard to recognise and repair the damaged boundaries in our own relationships.

Damaged boundaries create unhealthy relationships.

Personal Experience: For most of my life I believed that it was nice to give and not nice to take. Life taught me that this is not a balanced view. I learned about the four roles of Victims, Perpetrators, CareGivers and CareTakers from William Spear.

You may find reflecting on these distinct roles useful as I have. Without boundaries, we may become **Victims** in our relationships. Without boundaries, we may feel the need to act as aggressors or **Perpetrators** in our relationships, by encroaching on the boundaries of others and making them into our victims. Without boundaries, we may feel fearful, that we need to be taken care of, so that we lose our independence and personal power. In this role, we trade knowledge of our own power and independence for the role of **CareTaker**, taking or receiving care from others. The other side of this is that we may become **CareGivers**, where we put others in the role of **CareTakers**.

To summarise, we can restore boundaries by choosing not to be:
Victims – defending a weakened boundary and being mistreated and victimised by others
Perpetrators who victimise others to hide their own fear, pain or vulnerability
Care-Takers or takers of care – believing that we are anything but magnificent and complete and that we need others to take care of us before we can be whole
Care-Givers – giving to others in ways that leave them feeling anything but magnificent, powerful and whole.

You may like to consider where you can see examples of each of these roles occurring in your own relationships.

Returning to 'the beautiful garden of my mind', by defending the boundaries built around our pain, we keep the garden of our mind in ruin and ourselves in suffering. We need to clean up our garden, remove the defence mechanisms built on pain and replace them with healthy boundaries. With healthy boundaries we can preserve the integrity and beauty of our garden and begin to live with peace of mind.

Good fences make good neighbours.
Unless we can maintain our fences, we must become bad neighbours to survive.

As we bring order and integrity to our own lives and relationships, we support others in doing the same.

The garden is our mind, naturally still and clear and structured perfectly to serve our purpose, but it is disfigured by the paths that have been worn by avoiding debris of afflictive emotions – wherever it has fallen.

If we remove the mental debris, and tend the garden, nature will self-repair and all will find its proper place. Beautiful plants will naturally heal the scars left by past suffering and we will find it easy to see a new path, to follow our purpose, and to experience the joy, that comes with it.

Dodging all this mental debris is stressful.

In the absence of stress it is easier to be loving and compassionate.

In the absence of stress, it is easier to have free will in how we respond to circumstances, rather than reacting like one billiard ball that has been struck by another. On the other hand, debris and the work it takes to avoid the debris, leave us in a continual state of stress. Stress takes away our free will.

Suffering Cycle: Difficult Circumstances Produce Destructive Actions

Mental debris of afflictive emotions and damaged boundaries create the experience of stress.
Continual stress causes illness.
When we are stressed or ill, it is easy to follow afflictive emotions.
We may pass on difficult circumstances to others by taking destructive actions. We are more likely to create relationships that lack respect, support and power.

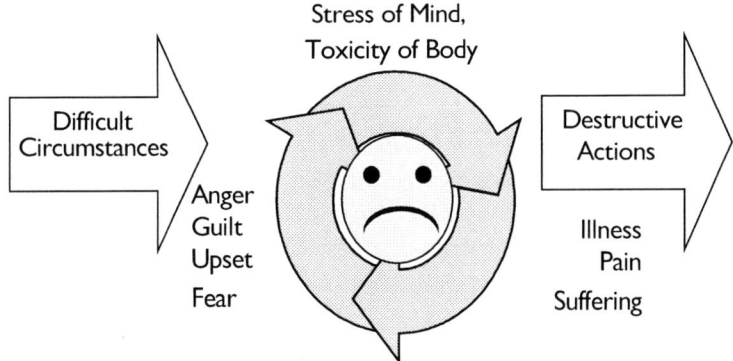

Figure 6: The Suffering Cycle

Living in the Suffering Cycle creates a life of suffering and stress.

If we can manage and eliminate stress, it is easier to 'stay on the mark' and choose to be a more shining example of a human being. When our mind is a beautiful garden with clear, well-maintained boundaries, we can follow our purpose without being distracted by stress, anger, guilt, upset, and fear. Instead of reacting, we can choose to make different choices.

> **Personal Experience**: I notice that whenever I respond to difficult circumstances with afflictive emotions, it bounces back on me. Problems seem to escalate.

Transforming Cycle: Difficult Circumstances Produce Constructive Actions

A clear mind and clear boundaries let us respond from free will. Choosing to respond from free will lets us retain our peace of mind and physical body

balance.

When we have free will and body balance, we can experience sustained wellness, vitality and joy.

We can transform difficult circumstances with constructive actions and build respectful, powerful and supportive relationships.

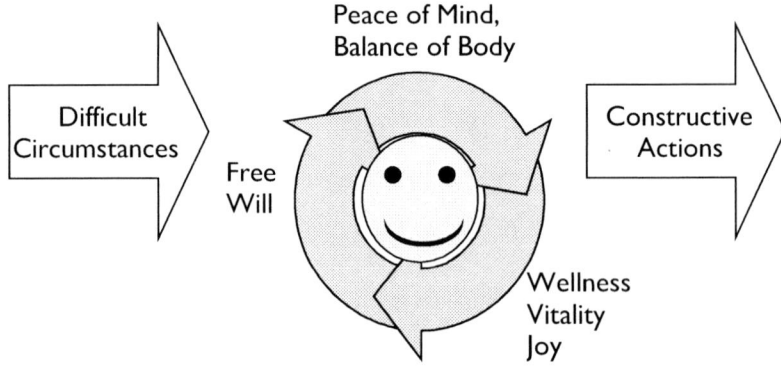

Figure 7: The Transforming Cycle

Living in the Transforming Cycle creates a life of joy and vitality.

When our mind is a beautiful garden with clear, healthy boundaries, we can experience the peace of mind and the bliss of being on purpose.

Personal Experience: I notice that whenever I respond to difficult circumstances with love and compassion, problems seem to dissolve. To respond with love and compassion, I have to recognise and resolve my own issues and I grow in the process. When I act out of afflictive emotion, I aim to correct the consequences as quickly as possible.

Mahatma Gandhi advocated the transformation of difficult circumstances into constructive actions through non-violence. In 1939 he said:

"I am an irrepressible optimist. My optimism rests on my belief in the infinite possibilities of the individual to develop non-violence. The more you develop it in your own being, the more infectious it becomes till it overwhelms your surroundings and by and by might over sweep the world".

Non-violence is about ending the Suffering Cycle, by choosing not to react to difficult circumstances like a billiard ball, but to exercise free will in choosing constructive actions.

"Turn the other cheek" can be understood to mean "Respond to the difficult circumstances of a slap on the cheek by choosing to take constructive actions, rather than simply reacting by slapping back. Better to turn the cheek and consider the right response than to slap back and think later."

"Turn the other cheek" can also be understood to mean, "When you are a Zen Archer and miss the mark, do not stamp your feet, just still the mind, realign" and then take action. Alternatively, we can understand "turn the other cheek" to mean: if you are a gardener and someone damages your garden, repair the fence and the damage that was done. Do not just build a fence around the damage or fight the people who did the damage and make the problem worse.

Toxic debris in the beautiful garden of our body

If our lives are stressed and we are challenged with difficult circumstances, then we may not have the personal resources to 'deal with' issues as they happen. Instead, we may leave the debris in the garden of our mind and the damage to our boundaries. Mentally and emotionally, we become stressed. At a chemical level our body behaves in a similar way to our mind. It cleans up debris of acid toxins when it can, but stores excess toxins away for later if it cannot deal with them. When the body stores up too much debris over time, we see the result in low energy and vitality, loss of flexibility, weight gain, arthritis, clogged arteries and other illnesses.

In the absence of persistent stress our body can go to work on repairing itself and keeping us fit and well with vitality and energy. At a cellular, biochemical, (or body chemical) level, being overweight, having arthritis and gout are all made more likely by the stress that creates an acid environment in the body. As we reduce our stress level, we lower the level of acidity in our bodies. This allows the toxic acidic debris that contributes to these illnesses to be dissolved and removed.

So, as we remove debris from the garden of our mind, by eliminating stressful thought patterns, we help to remove toxic debris from our cells by reducing the acidity of our bodies.

This toxic debris includes the fatty acids that deposit as body fat, the uric acid that deposits in the joints as painful gout and the acid toxins that cause arthritis. Removing stress helps the body to get well and stay well.

As we remove chemical toxins from our body it is easier to think clearly. Headaches and other pains may subside. When we are free from pain it is

easier to let go of anger, forgive and release guilt, upset and stress.

Creating the beautiful garden

As well as mentally detoxifying by removing mental debris, we can physically detoxify by reducing or eliminating our intake of foods that make our bodies toxic.

Personal Experience: Coming from a family of medics and having opted out of the medical course at Oxford when I was 18, I have grown sceptical of the ability of conventional medicine alone to address the health and happiness challenges that we face individually and as a global community. Over the last 20 years, I have continually tried to learn and adapt my own diet and exercise practices. In the process I have come to see health from a more holistic perspective. I believe that western medicine is being forced to take on board the same transformation as science and business: from parts-based thinking to holistic thinking. As a result of years of experimentation and improvement I am quite rigorous in my diet practices now. I notice the effect of different foods and drugs (like coffee) on my body. In life, I am fairly consistently well and happy and have not taken antibiotics for over 20 years. When I do eat or drink certain things, I notice the impact on my ability to respond to life without afflictive emotion. I do not believe that there is one right health regime for all people and I am not an expert on how other people need to eat, drink or exercise. I do perceive a powerful link between health and exercise habits and, for example, intuition and afflictive emotion. I believe that when as people and societies we eat manufactured foods grown and processed with chemicals, we stress our bodies and it is harder to act without afflictive emotions. If we eat modern processed and chemical foods we are likely to be more stressed and it is harder to be intuitive, forgiving, compassionate and loving. At the time of writing this, in the spirit of openness, I have shared some of my current diet and exercise practices as an appendix to this book. They are not intended as a prescription for anyone else!

Stress results from the build-up of adrenaline in the body over time. Our bodies naturally produce adrenaline at times of fear and excitement. Adrenaline gives us access to immediate resources of energy to help us to fight or run. Adrenaline was a useful resource when survival depended on the ability of our ancestors to run from a predator, or chase their prey. Today the situation has completely reversed.

Survival depends at an individual and social level on our ability to make calm choices that we will not regret.

For example today, we have continual access to potentially dangerous equipment like cars and knives. In a moment of acting out of fear, a moment of anger, we can easily cause harm to ourselves or another person. Stress – the prolonged build-up of adrenaline – makes us more prone to immediate outbursts of fear or anger. Adrenaline provides our body with immediate energy when it is needed.

The adrenaline production, which evolved to save early ancestors from predators, is now the source of stress, which over time kills so many people, through the heart attacks, cancer and other illnesses that it promotes.

As well as through illness, stress damages people through the rash things that we say and actions that we take when we are stressed.

Good people are likely to behave badly when stressed – damaging themselves and others.

Across society, the implications of this insight are even more significant. Individuals have the ability to start and end trade wars, forgive or enforce repayment of third world debt and even to take whole continents to war.

When we are willing to deal with the debris in our own minds, we can tend our own physical and mental gardens and reclaim our free will. With free will, we can most effectively play our part in creating and owning a future to be proud of.

Without the ability to manage our own stress, it is hard for us to act from free will because we do not have the mental stillness for clear thinking.

Blame and guilt drive deep stakes into the garden of our mind, holding the mechanical debris of incomplete emotions in place. It is hard or impossible to forgive, give up, let go, in the billiard ball paradigm where I have no free will about the way that I feel. If I am angry because of someone else – like a machine reacting – then I may require that person to change in order to clear my anger.

When I am committed to clearing the garden of my mind, to forgive, to let go, to give up, so as to be free from afflictive emotion, I can forgive anything.

I can achieve peace of mind and make good choices about how to do my best as a person, a parent and a citizen. I can have free will.

Why would we want to take on dismantling the knot of afflictive emotions that governs our actions for so much of the time? Why not just put up with them? Because rather than creating improvement, afflictive emotions steal our free will and maintain suffering in our lives and the world, In personal, family, social or business life, these emotions are very costly unless they are managed responsibly. They may make us feel justified, but they are often damaging. How can I know how to speak to my child, what to say, if I am controlled by anger, by guilt, by upset or by fear?

Blame, guilt and anger result from a perception of a situation or life. One reaction to a child stealing money might be anger and blame. Knowing that the child was stealing to buy medicine for a sick parent or to feed a hungry brother or sister might change our perception in an instant.

So, are afflictive emotions just an unfortunate mistake in our human design? Before we discard afflictive emotions for their cost to human happiness and our future survival, let us ask: what can afflictive emotions teach us about getting back on the mark?

11. Learning from afflictive emotions

If we were to get angry about being angry, or upset about being upset, or guilty about our guilt, we would be judging, reacting and missing the gift in these emotions.

The gift in afflictive emotions is that they teach us about our boundaries. Something has happened that was not OK.

What happened?

Does the boundary need to be respected, supported and strengthened, or dismantled and removed?

This is a powerful question for revealing the gift in afflictive emotions.

Is the boundary in the garden of our mind a flowerbed that must be protected or debris that must be cleared?

Afflictive emotions provide a constant feedback to allow us to grow and evolve towards perfection.

If, in our commitment to change our world, we react out of afflictive emotion, we become a part of the Suffering Cycle, a part of the problem, not part of the solution.

The word 'manifest' means to make real to make tangible, to bring into existence.

If, in our commitment to forgiveness, we accept the role of victim, we erode our ability to manifest and change our world.

When we forgive, we must understand what we are forgiving. What do we need to do to preserve and protect the boundaries to stop it from happening again? We must protect the flowerbeds of our garden for they are the source of our beauty and power, through which we bring beauty into our world.

If we do not protect the boundaries of our flowerbeds, we are likely to lose ground over time, until we have no ground in our garden.

Forgiving while maintaining and creating boundaries

Ideally, we can forgive, **and** when we forgive, we maintain and strengthen our boundaries, ensuring that a situation that required forgiveness will not happen again.

Personal Experience: In 1995, having experienced painful guilt, I made a kind of karmic contract. I took on the belief that anger is an attempt to make someone else feel guilty. I was feeling guilty. Someone was angry with me. It was unbearable. I realised that I could not change their anger, but I could change myself.

I gave up the right to get angry. By promising not to make anyone else feel guilt, by being angry, I was somehow released from the burden of the guilt. Giving up the right to anger released joy and love in my life. I still aspire to this same standard. However, when I do experience anger, I don't ignore it without consideration. I try to forgive it **and** to understand its source. Do I need to strengthen a boundary so that this will not happen again? I now believe that I must develop the combination of forgiveness and boundaries to allow me to be happy and effective in the world.

The chart below suggests that we can be both strong on forgiveness and strong on maintaining boundaries.

Part I: Purpose and Vision

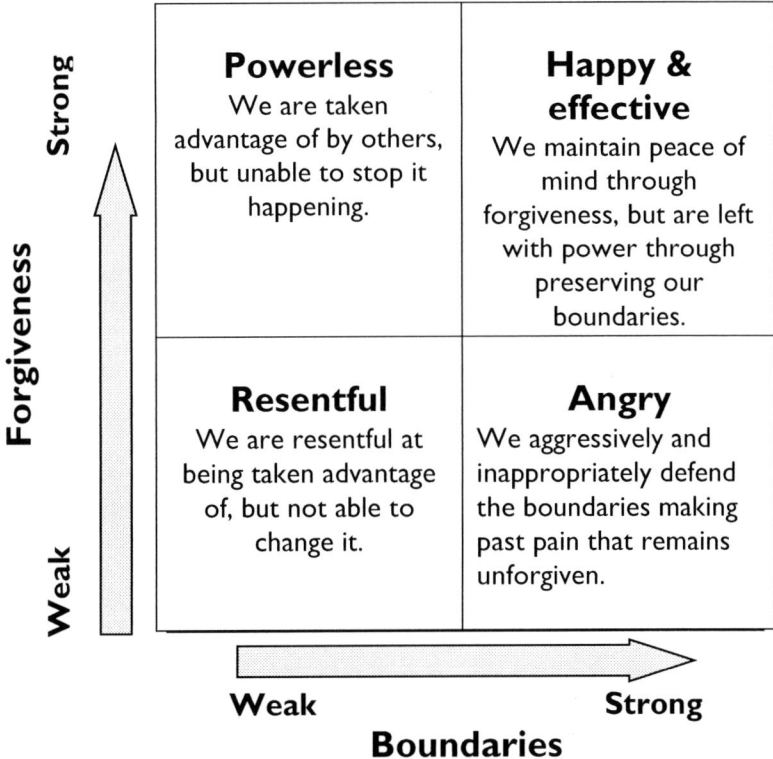

Figure 8: Combining Forgiveness and Boundaries

Use Exercise 8. ❦ Reflect on forgiveness and boundaries ❦ on page 130, to explore your experience combining forgiveness and boundaries.

When we seek to forgive, we must not be seduced by the idea that someone else has to change for our lives to get better. When we forgive, we become a part of the solution. This does not mean that we allow others to violate our boundaries.

If the anger is still there, how do you know that you are reacting to the violation of a boundary? Could it be that the other person has just touched debris in your garden - an old wound?

One way to give up afflictive emotion is to develop compassion. This is a technique that you can use and cultivate, into a habit. See Exercise 9. **Giving up afflictive emotion by choosing compassion** on page 130.

Compassion works because it gives access to a meaning that is not afflictive. The first step is to realise:

The event is not personal – it just happened and means nothing.

The event has no meaning without the meaning that you give it. The next step is to realise that at a deeper level:

The event is deeply personal tuition from the Universe to set you back on the mark.

Everything that happened is a gift to support your growth. Judgement – imposing a meaning – does not work, because it tries to impose meaning on the situation rather than understanding the meaning within the situation. The more compassion we have, the more we can understand and the more we can find a more useful meaning in a situation.

See page 67 in 16 below, Karma: the gift of free tuition.

See Exercise 19 ✿**Surrendering to love: the easiest way to learn life's lessons**✿ on page 147.

We have found the meaning in a situation when we understand how it helps us to learn and grow and get back on the mark.

The Forgiveness Spring-Clean provides a structure for systematically forgiving to clear the garden of your mind.

Suffering does not have to be unbearable or deadened by retreat from life.

We can maintain Internal Heaven in the garden of our minds and from this place of love and compassion, we can build perfection in the world around us. When we are living in Internal Heaven and building our dreams, the challenges and trials of suffering become fuel to our commitment.

We can change our minds by clearing away mental debris and stilling the mind with meditation to build Internal Heaven.

We can repair and build our boundaries, protecting the flowerbeds, to protect this heaven in our minds.

By repairing and protecting the boundaries in our relationships, we reclaim our power and with it our ability to manifest. By repairing and protecting the boundaries in our communities and in our world, we can build a beautiful garden in our world: a kind of Heaven on Earth.

When we are manifesting our dreams, we can live in Internal Heaven. As we live in Internal Heaven, we can build Heaven on Earth.

Spiritually, we forgive to preserve our Internal Heaven. We give of love and compassion unconditionally and maintain the garden of our mind free from anger and resentment.

Practically, mentally, materially, we create boundaries so that we do not diminish our ability to manifest in the world. By preserving our boundaries, we maintain and develop our ability and power to build the beautiful garden in our world.

Being able to give up afflictive emotions is a key to our spiritual and practical progress. How can we learn to give up afflictive emotions in an instant by choice, rather than just as a reaction to external information?

12. The gift of forgiveness

There is a tight relationship between fault, blame, anger, guilt and upset. If we can unpick any part of this knot, we can untie the knot and start to regain our peace of mind and free will. We have free will when we can act from choice, rather than as an unchosen reaction to circumstances around us.

Forgiveness is the key to peace of mind.

To forgive is to give up anger, blame and judgement, to give up resentment and any desire to punish, to give as before. If you are *just willing* to give up the afflictive emotions attached to an issue, you may find that this is enough to dissolve the afflictive emotion. You can then choose, based on free will, what you need to do or say to complete the situation. We naturally feel lightened up when we forgive or give up anger. Forgiving some things takes great courage. Following are some useful tools for forgiving.

Celebrate every act of forgiveness or letting go as a step towards freedom.

You can become an expert at forgiving by practising on the easy issues. From these, work up to the more challenging issues that can give you the most freedom when they are resolved.

It helps to realise that anger, guilt, upset and fear are our own emotions, so we have the choice to give up and let go, without needing anything from anyone else. The following exercises can be understood at 3 levels:

- At a psychological level as a way of communicating with the subconscious;
- At a metaphysical level as a way of invoking the support of the Universe;
- At a scientific level as a way of shaping the field of consciousness;
- Or at a spiritual level as a way of invoking the support of angelic helpers or God.

The point is that these exercises work if you are willing to have them work. It is up to us whether we choose to think of this as a psychological, metaphysical or spiritual exercise. Knowing that it would be good to forgive is not the same as forgiving. Do what works for you to actually forgive. If a purely intellectual approach has not worked to date, be open-minded enough to try something more psychological, metaphysical or spiritual.

How to stop acting out of afflictive emotions

To live our purpose, we need to be able to master afflictive emotions like guilt and anger, so that they do not drive our actions, stealing our free will.

The test of greatness and free will is not whether we get angry and guilty or not, but how long we stay that way and whether we act out of these afflictive emotions.

Personal experience with the exercises: The key exercise for this chapter is the Forgiveness Spring-clean. When working through the exercises thoroughly and systematically, I found this spring-clean powerful and lightening. Brainstorming issues to forgive, I listed issues that I really wasn't aware of until the exercise. The simple ritual allowed me to release most of the issues. There were a few issues, where I could feel, during the ritual that I needed to do something more. That is where I used other approaches like 'forgiving through grace' and 'writing and burning a letter'.

For example, I found that I wrote a letter to God who I already felt I had a good relationship with and also a letter to my father who died in 1969. Burning these letters and placing the ash at the roots of an apple tree was a very beautiful and powerful experience. The overall Forgiveness Spring-clean is a powerful process which I very much recommend. It was particularly powerful following the Purpose exercise and other earlier exercises which I did in turn.

The key Exercise for this chapter is the Forgiveness Spring Clean. As a part of your spring clean, you may use some of the other Forgiveness Exercises. Briefly review the following Exercises, before starting *Life Change 3. Forgiveness spring-clean* on page 138.

Forgiving *through Grace* on page 132.

Forgiving a lifelong issue by writing and burning a letter on page 133.

Letting go of guilt: forgiving myself on page 134.

Letting go of anger: forgiving others on page 135.

Simply forgiving an innocent child on page 137.

Giving up guilt as an innocent child on page 137.

Reclaiming peace of mind on page 138.

To forgive and systematically clear the garden of your mind, try *Life Change 3. Forgiveness spring-clean* on page 138. You will never know what a difference it could make unless you do it. In this exercise, you systematically give up all the things you are angry about and all the things for which you feel guilty. Most of us have 'baggage' of unforgiven issues, so don't focus on how much there is to be done, but rather on how far you have come.

You can use the **Forgiveness spring-clean** repeatedly – think of it like regular cleaning. Every time you clean, everything gets a little bit cleaner.

Forgiving more over time

Whenever a forgiven item comes to mind, check whether you feel any afflictive emotions over it. If you do not feel afflictive emotion, then smile and enjoy the fact that you have forgiven it. If you do feel afflictive emotion, you can use one of the approaches above to forgive. Think of it as a project to spring-clean your life.

A useful way to get started is to prioritise the issues to forgive based on which ones will give you the most energy back compared to the energy which must be invested to complete them. (Pick the 'low hanging fruit' first, so that you have a taste for it and an incentive to go on to pick the juicier fruits which are harder to reach.)

13. Freedom from stress

Stress is the build-up of debris in the mind, toxins in the cells and tension in the body. Our experience of stress may grow when we have too much to do in too little time

With our minds trained in the logic of billiard ball cause and effect, we forget that every aspect of our body is regulated by our conscious and subconscious mind. From one perspective, it is very strange that we think we need to take drugs to lower the blood pressure, or reduce the heart rate, when somewhere down there, our subconscious mind is controlling all our body functions. The chemicals and drugs we put into our body to try to control stress can create problems as well as solving them.

It is not surprising that by putting a pill in the stomach, we can affect the pressure of the blood. It is no more surprising that by regulating the thoughts in our mind, we can affect the pressure of our blood, the acidity of our stomach and tissue and many other measures of stress, health and well-being.

Stress can seem to be a monster that otherwise powerful people cannot control. It is true that we cannot shout at stress, or frighten stress to go away, but across everything we think and do, we have abundant opportunities to dissolve and eliminate stress.

In this world where life and work pull for stress, to make good judgements and produce results we must manage our stress. We can learn to manage stress and it can be easy, we just have to be willing to choose appropriate habits.

Body intake habits: food, drink and water

Everyone is different. There are many diets, exercises and approaches to health. Over time, we take in foods and drinks that make our body acid and toxic. To keep the life-giving balance at all cost, our body deposits fatty acids (as fat), uric acid (resulting in gout for example) and other acid toxins (resulting in for example arthritis). Over time these toxins build up in our body contributing to tiredness, stress, irritability and degenerative illness. By taking care of what we eat and drink and of the air we breathe, with every drink, with every meal, with every breath, we can be maintaining balance and cleansing our body.

If we follow the trends of the developed world and continue to eat more processed foods, sugar, chemical additives, meat, etc., we are likely to play our part in the statistics of growing physical, emotional and mental sickness of the developed world.

Body care, exercise, stress, adrenaline, toxins and the immune system

Personal Experience: When I was in my early 20s, I travelled frequently to Grenoble in France as part of the research project I was working on. The hotel where I stayed served extremely rich food, which I enjoyed and ate in excess. On returning from one trip, I was debilitated with pain in my stomach and extremely weak. I knew that I had overdone it. That was a turning point. I decided that I wanted to be healthy and well more than I wanted to eat luxury food. After years of refinement and change, some of my current diet habits are listed in III. Personal Diet Practices on page 194.

A healthy body supports a healthy mind. Exercise metabolises (burns) away the adrenaline that results in stress. Exercise warms up the body and helps to dissolve the toxins that have been deposited over time.

- Vigorous exercise burns up the unused adrenaline that results in stress. Removing adrenaline gives our body a chance to relax and do housekeeping. When the adrenaline is gone, our immune system, (body protection and repair system), is active. When adrenaline is present, our immune system is suppressed and inactive. Adrenaline may put us in a good position to fight off a predator, but it will not help us to fight off a cold! A stressful life suppresses our immune system and makes us prone to illness. Regular vigorous exercise activates our immune system, helping us to stay well.

- Vigorous exercise also gets the blood moving and warms the body, dissolving toxins lodged in the cells. During and after exercise, drinking good quality water helps to flush out toxins before they are deposited back in our body tissues.

Personal Experience: As well as running, walking, roller-skating and occasional gym exercise, which I do in moderation, I find practising Kundalini Yoga particularly valuable for health, life balance and intuition.

Mind care: De-stressing habits

Our mind is continually reinforcing stress or peace of mind. The thoughts that we choose determine our level of stress and hence our degree of free will and, over time, our level of vitality, health and ultimately our length of life.

Find a method of meditating or a yoga that gives you profound relaxation, dissolving stress and giving an experience of oneness. Experiment with doing this practice once or twice a day.

Mind care: giving up worry

The following steps are based on advice from the Dalai Lama in his book "Ancient Wisdom Modern World".

List all the issues that you are worried about and all the things you have to do on a piece of paper. For each item, answer the following:

Can I do anything to affect this?

If you can and you choose to do it, plan to do what you can do and let go of the worry because you are doing what you can do.

If you can and you choose not to do it, let go of the worry, because you have chosen not to act.

If you can't, then let go of the worry because there is nothing that you can do by worrying.

For links to body and mind care sites, products and services, visit: WWW.MindOfMany.COM.

14. The measure of greatness

Today the measure of greatness is whether we have the courage to know and live our purpose. Do we have the self-discipline to forgo knee-jerk reactions driven by afflictive emotion? Do we choose the habits that eliminate stress?

When to speak and when to be silent

When we have peace of mind, we can trust what we choose to say. When we are angry, upset, fearful, guilty, we may regret whatever we say. For example, should a parent shout at their child just because the parent is upset, for example when the child has an accident?

Communication in itself is a wonderful thing, but every communication has effects and implications beyond the moment. An angry word to another can create mental debris of guilt, fear or anger, damaging the person we communicate with and the people they come into contact with for years to come. But if we don't 'speak our mind', how else can we get issues and upsets 'off our chest'? When we speak out of anger or upset, we give up ownership of our future, we are controlled by the past – by the issue, problem or injustice, which preceded the strong emotion. If we are to do better than the child who says: "now look what you have made me do," then we need to manage difficult communications without being controlled by afflictive emotion. This requires serenity and peace of mind.

There are two ways in which we can own the future, even when afflictive emotion is present:

- If we are able, diffuse or complete the afflictive emotion for ourselves before we act, or to borrow Gandhi's words to 'practise non-violence'. This is a contribution and positive example to people around us.
- Otherwise, communicate or act in such a way that we acknowledge the presence of our afflictive emotion, but do not blame anyone else for it. When we do this, we distance ourselves from the afflictive emotion so that we manage or own it, rather than it managing or controlling us.

The bad news is that afflictive emotions steal free will from all of us sometimes. At these times, the measure of our greatness is how long we allow afflictive emotions to drive our action before we stop reacting and start to clear up any mess we have made.

Part I: Purpose and Vision

After an angry word we may feel righteous and justified. In that moment, we lost our free will; we no longer had clear choice in what we did. Often, with hindsight, we realise that the righteous feeling deceived us into doing or saying something that we are not proud of. On the other hand we may feel guilty – another afflictive emotion. Better to use one of the tools described earlier in this book to 'let go' and forgive before acting in haste.

To play a part in creating a future worth choosing we must become better and better at completing our own afflictive emotion, before anyone else is affected by it. We must become better at communicating responsibly, even when afflictive emotions try to claim control and we must become better at reclaiming the future from afflictive emotions quickly whenever we lose it.

If we compare ourselves to the Zen Archer, when we release the arrow while controlled by afflictive emotion, the arrow misses the target. Missing the target was the original meaning of sin. Any guilt and sense of wrongdoing and badness were added by successive human translations of early texts. The early texts had a simple practical message to help people to behave in a way they could be proud of. Later translations forgot the analogy of the archer and with it the absence of judgement.

When we notice that the arrow has missed its target, we may be tempted by afflictive emotions. Repentance is to understand that we are 'off the mark' in such a way as to naturally correct. This means noticing that our future is owned by afflictive emotion and reclaiming it.

The measure of our greatness as a parent, a partner, a colleague, a leader is not whether we are sometimes 'off the mark', but how quickly we recognise it and get back on the mark again.

When we know our purpose and live by it and when we can maintain our free will, our ability to choose, even through the turbulence of afflictive emotion, then we have powerful ingredients for living a life of joy and making our contribution to the Emerging Global Transformation.

15. Reality before it happens

The beauty and perfection of our human body unfolds from a single cell. At the moment of fertilisation, the blueprint of the child is already present, but only in the unmanifest world and not in the physical or manifest world. The physicist David Bohm named the unmanifest world from which reality unfolds as the **Implicate Order**. The future is implied, but not yet real. He named the unfolded, 'real', manifest world that we can see, hear, touch and smell the **Explicate Order**.

Personal Experience: I am deeply grateful to the late physicist David Bohm, a beautiful, gentle soul who opened my mind to understanding the unseen world that we touch through intuition. It was David who first described the Zen Archer to me in the early 1980s. I remember at the time feeling that the Implicate and Explicate Orders that he was describing must apply to organisations. Now this understanding provides a foundation from which I understand organisational transformation.

The reality that we perceive with our senses unfolds from a blueprint, a pattern that we can perceive through our intuition.

Reality unfolds from the Implicate Order. If we struggle with circumstances rather than working consciously or unconsciously on the Implicate Order, we are likely to suffer disappointment.

Our role can be to unfold the Emerging Global Transformation from implicate possibility into our thoughts and through our actions, into reality.

When we still our mind through meditation our intuition begins to perceive this pattern or blueprint – the Implicate Order. Synchronicity – meaningful coincidence gives us clues to the underlying pattern of the Implicate Order. Our intuition allows us to understand and see the deeper patterns behind what is and what will be.

By developing our intuition we begin to perceive the pattern of the Emerging Global Transformation in everything.

The same acorn may unfold into a different oak tree given different circumstances. As we develop our intuition, we begin to see the pattern. The way that we use what we see determines whether the acorn will grow into an oak tree and how it will grow.

We are custodians of the future, not victims of the future. The future holds wonderful possibility. It is up to us whether we make that future real.

We affect the Implicate Order when we successfully wish, pray, will or intend so that reality unfolds to reflect our intention. Our wish, prayer, will or intention is then an act of *causation*.

Acts of causation can carry great power. Making a commitment can be an act of causation.

"Until one is committed, there is hesitancy, the chance to draw back, always ineffectiveness. Concerning all acts of initiative (and creation),

there is one elementary truth the ignorance of which kills countless ideas and splendid plans: that the moment one definitely commits oneself, then providence moves too.
All sorts of things occur to help one that would never otherwise have occurred. A whole stream of events issues from the decision raising in one's favour all manner of unforeseen incidents and meetings and material assistance which no man could have dreamed would have come his way."

Taken from the Scottish Himalayan Expedition, by W.H. Murray.

Acts of causation such as promises and commitments are like a magnet, aligning the implicate order to deliver what is promised or committed.

To the extent that we have made a commitment that has led to extraordinary results, or even 'miracles' we are familiar with our power of causation.

With power comes responsibility

We keep our children away from potentially dangerous tools. As adults we do not play with knives and guns because while they are powerful, they are also dangerous. When we **do** something, we 'flap a butterfly wing' at the physical level, resulting in consequences and repercussions. For example, when we slam a door or break something in anger there are physical consequences. If our actions can have powerful consequences, what about acts of causation for example vows, intentions and commitments.

Just as we do not allow our children to play with certain things because we believe them to be dangerous, so many traditions, religions and spiritual teachings have withheld information from people relating to causation because of the consequences of misuse. Before we let the child play with the tool we make sure that they understand it. Before we fly a helicopter we make sure we know how to fly it and know the consequences of potential actions.

Causative acts are actions that affect the Implicate Order. They unfold into the Explicate Order of thoughts and physical consequences. This is very powerful. Why would we not just learn to always act at a causative level? Is there some responsibility that comes with the power? Is causation like a knife or a gun – both powerful and potentially dangerous?

To safely use the power of causation, we must be aware of the consequences of our actions and how the consequences we create for others reflect back in consequences for ourselves.

For books and links to experimental evidence of the power of intention, prayer and alignment, visit: WW.MindOfMany.COM.

16. Karma: the gift of free tuition

To consider the consequences and responsibilities that come with power, let us return to the Zen Archer and then delve into the depths of cause and effect. Newton identified a simple cause and effect in physical things, which we now describe in the laws of mechanics. Strike one billiard ball against another and it will cause the other to move. Newton's Third Law: Action and reaction are equal and opposite. You can't touch without being touched.

Spiritually we interpret Newton's Third Law as meaning that our actions have equal consequences. We reap what we sow.

Heisenberg discovered a deeper level of cause and effect in the Uncertainty Principle that shows that whatever we **observe**, we impact.

Spiritually, we interpret Heisenberg's Uncertainty Principle as meaning that whenever we perceive anything with our sight, sound, smell or touch, we affect it.

The same is true at a mental level. Whenever we perceive and judge something, it is an act of thought and impacts the thing that we are judging. We can never be bystanders in life because we affect whatever we perceive. When our mind is full of thoughts about things and people, these thoughts have impact. The other side of this is that whatever does the measuring is also impacted by the act of measuring.

In a world where our thoughts and intentions have power and we reap what we sow, it is important to have clear, positive thoughts and intentions.

Spiritually, we interpret this as meaning: our actions and judgements that affect others will also affect us.

What goes around comes around! This law of cause and effect applied to human motivation, intention, thought and action is also known by the name of karma.

Another consequence of Heisenberg's Uncertainty Principle is that it is impossible to know both the speed and position of an electron. Spiritually, we interpret this as meaning that we can never know everything about anything.

We are wise to suspend judgement, knowing that whatever we believe we know is only part of the truth.

In **Chapter 18. Knowledge and compassion** on page 78, we explore this insight further. Before we go there, why should we want to know about karma?

16% of people said that the one question they would ask a Supreme Being if they could get a direct and immediate answer would be: "Why do bad things happen?"

USA Today, survey from the Lutheran Brotherhood.

(Remember that 34% asked, "What is my purpose here?")

The other side to this is the question:

"Why do good things happen?"

Understanding karma provides a simple, empowering way for us to answer these questions for ourselves.

When we intend, think, speak or act in life from fear or anger and wish suffering on others, we accumulate negative karma. Sooner or later, we reap suffering in our lives.

When we intend, think, speak, act in life from love and compassion, we accumulate positive karma. Sooner or later, we reap satisfaction and happiness in our lives.

Referring back, to "**The beautiful garden of my mind**" on page 37 in Section 10 above:

The Suffering Cycle builds negative karma, whereas the Transforming Cycle eliminates negative karma and creates positive karma.

In the terms described above: In a challenging and sometimes stressful world, how can we stay on purpose and play our part in the Emerging Global Transformation. In **The Zen Archer: aligning with purpose**, karma helps us to learn which intentions and actions are on target and which are not. Just as the child learns what is safe from the hot pan or the sharp knife, karma helps to teach us which actions are spiritually safe ('on the mark') and which actions are not safe ('off the mark').

There is no judgement in karma, just a simple natural feedback, just as there is no judgement in the hot pan or the sharp knife.

Karma provides the feedback by which the Zen Archer can see the target after she releases the arrow.

When burned by the hot pan, the child may be angry at the pan, its parent, everything. Unfortunately, this afflictive emotion is likely to lead to more trouble, not less. In the same way, if we as adults 'miss the mark' by speaking angry words, driven from afflictive emotion, rather than free will, we may find those angry words reflected back in angry words, actions, and undesirable consequences. Consider the Zen Archer. If she were to angrily stamp her feet, look away from the target and release another arrow, we would not expect her to be on the mark. The Zen Archer calmed her mind to restore her equilibrium, before realigning with the target and releasing another arrow.

To get back on the mark spiritually, we must learn to respond to difficult situations without 'stamping our feet', that is without reacting from afflictive emotion.

Karma teaches us to choose the Transforming Cycle rather than the Suffering Cycle.

Karma is the ultimate teacher of free will, personal growth and of how to recognise and create a future worth choosing. Just as gravity never fails, karma never fails.

If we respond to circumstances by shouting and stamping, then we get further from the mark and will likely have more work to do to find the mark again. This compounding and storing-up of 'off the markness' has sometimes been understood as vengefulness on the part of the Universe or God, fuelling guilt and fear. We can now see clearly that if the Zen Archer thought that God was angry with her, she would likely miss the target again.

Generally, missing the mark, (or acting inconsistently with our purpose or against the good of other people or nature), is unpleasant in the long term, if not in the short term.

Off the mark intentions, thoughts and actions may sometimes lead to power, influence and wealth, but not to the peace of mind that comes from being 'on the mark' and the joy that comes from being on purpose.

Freedom from suffering comes from on-the-mark intentions, thoughts, words and actions.

We might expect that a vengeful Universe might punish the Zen Archer for missing the mark, but karma is a law, like gravity, not a personality.

Karma is not a personality that favours or punishes, but a law, like gravity.

Karma does not prescribe how long or how hard we must toil to get back on the mark, only that when our arrow is pointing away from the target, we will miss. Translating this into our own lives, karma does not mean that we need to suffer for releasing an arrow in the wrong direction, only that our arrow will miss the target (which may have consequences) and that if we want to be on the mark in future, we must adjust. What we do in intention, thought and action will have physical and mental consequences.

When we act from afflictive emotion, with the intent to harm others, or without consideration or compassion, we may create suffering for others. Karma does not say that we must be punished for making others suffer. However we must ultimately understand the impact of what we have done and at some level redress the blemish that it has caused, if we are to get back on the mark ourselves.

To get back on the mark, we need to learn compassion. One way to learn compassion for the way our actions have made others suffer is to suffer in a similar way. To grow spiritually, we must get back on the mark. The easiest way to do this may be to suffer.

Karma does not mean that our destiny is mapped out, only that at any point we are on or off the mark in certain ways.

Karma is the Universal gravity that relentlessly pulls us back to the mark.

Since our perceptions and intentions are powerful, they have powerful karmic consequences.

To summarise:
- If our motivation, intention, action or pleasure is to cause suffering, then we are off the mark and soon enough, the gravity of karma will act to bring us back to the mark. We can recognise that we are off the mark at any time. Then we can begin to remedy what we have intended, thought or done.
- If our motivation to act is from love and compassion and designed to eliminate suffering, the karmic consequences are positive. If our action is taken with positive intent, the karmic consequences will be positive. If we take pleasure in the happiness of others, the karmic consequences will be positive.

At any time, we can change the choices we make to eliminate negative karma and accumulate positive karma.

Although many of us do not know karma by name, we still have the feeling that when we cause suffering, we must in some way learn and grow before we can be released from what we have done. We have all practised thinking and doing and we understand that thoughts and actions have consequences. Now we recognise that practical consequences are just one aspect of the deeper karmic consequences.

When we follow our purpose and do what we came here to do with love, courage, humility and compassion, we clear negative karma and build positive karma.

When we cause suffering, we get more off the mark, leaving more mess to clear up – more spiritual learning to be done, more getting back on the mark and potentially more suffering to get there.

Karma does not mean that we have no free will.

Karma defines the mountains that we must cross to grow and develop spiritually.

We have the choice as to how and when we will cross these mountains and as a consequence how much joy or suffering we will experience in the crossing.

As we recognise karma, we become partners with the Universe in our own growth and transformation, recognising challenges as opportunities for insight and growth.

Personal Experience with Exercises: The exercises for this chapter ask whether by appreciating karma, you have become more able to:
1. live your purpose;
2. be more courageous when faced by similar challenges;
3. establish clear and healthy boundaries in relationships;
4. forgive others for a weakness that you demonstrated when meeting this challenge;
5. be compassionate and understanding to others who suffer similar circumstances to those that you suffered;
6. give love to others who experience a similar challenge;
7. or accept that you are more authentically powerful than you previously knew?

I found that, as a result of completing each of the exercises in this book, thoroughly and sequentially, my answer to all of these was YES. This was a surprise to me. I had no idea how much I would learn from doing the exercises.

If you would like to explore the certainty and confidence that comes from knowing and working with karma, the following two exercises are simple and effective.
Recognising karma on page 144 and
Learning from karma on page 145.

17. Surrendering to love

**My heart has become capable of every form:
It is a pasture for gazelles
And a monastery for Christian monks
And a temple for idols
And a Kaaba of the Pilgrim
And the tablets of the Torah
And the book of the Koran.
I follow the religion of love.
Whatever path love's camel takes,
this is my religion and my faith.**

Cheikh Mohieddine Ibn Arabi in the 12th century

There are many stories of people who make a wish and regret it when the wish has been granted, for example, Midas did not enjoy the consequences of his wish Everything he touched turned to gold, whether he liked it or not.

Working with the power of intention is not for fulfilling our greed. It is for fulfilling our purpose, growing spiritually and serving the Universe and the Emerging Global Transformation. We can reach a place from which to work powerfully with intention through relaxation, meditation or prayer. This is how we can create patterns of intention that unfold into reality.

We then affect the Implicate Order, the pattern and the blueprint from which reality unfolds. If we are to work powerfully with intention, we must be sure that our intentions, our motivations and our actions are 'on the mark'; that they are for the good of all concerned. To stay on the mark we must be masters of our afflictive emotion.

When we work with the power of intention, our actions have greater power and the karmic consequences are greater.

To safely use the power of our intention, we must be motivated with love and compassion. Love and compassion are not just things that we do. They are qualities of our being that can pervade our thoughts, words and actions.

When we sow the seeds of our actions with love, we reap the rewards of love. When we live our lives pervaded in love, we reap the rewards of bliss.

Giving of love, being in a loving state, blesses us. In the moment of giving love, we are in a kind of Internal Heaven. As the fruits of our intentions, thoughts and actions ripen, beauty unfolds into our world and we reap a kind of Heaven on Earth.

Karma is not something that happens, it is a force field that operates on everything all of the time. We can try to fight karma, or we can trust.

Over time, by continually correcting our unloving thoughts, words and actions, karma softens and dissolves us in a spiritual cleansing so that all that remains is love.

We can invite this spiritual cleansing into our lives. To do this, we must make an act of faith and humility, surrendering the power of our mind to the mystery of love.

When we surrender to love, the unseen world aligns itself to our cleansing.

We experience the same guided, accelerated transformation as the spiritual devotee who surrenders to the Universe or God. Miracles happen as the unseen world configures itself to teach and guide us, uninhibited by our control.

As we dare to surrender, we become love. Karma is taking us there anyway. When we surrender in humility, our mind and resources are used in the solution, without us having to understand how.

Our deep fear is that we might lose our identity as it is dissolved.

When we surrender the security of being a separate something with ego, opinions and boundaries, then we can come to know ourselves as everything: loving, compassionate and unbounded.

Through humility and surrender we come to embody the power and nobility of love.

To explore the peace that comes from surrendering to Love, try *Exercise 19. Surrendering to love: the easiest way to learn life's lessons* on page 147.

As we dare to surrender, we become love. Karma is taking us there anyway. When we surrender in humility, our mind and resources are used in the solution, without us having to understand how.

18. Knowledge and compassion

How can we gain knowledge of whatever lies beyond the bounds of our thought?

As we noted above in Chapter 16, **Karma: the gift of free tuition on page 67** above, Heisenberg's Uncertainty Principle states that we can never know the position and speed of an electron. From this, we have realised that as an external observer, we can never know everything about anything. In personal experience, if we can see what is being done, we cannot fully see why it is being done. We can only hope to rise above the level at which the action and intent exist, to understand the pattern of which they are both a part. In the case of the electron, at the level above detail, we can 'understand' that there is a relationship between position and speed. Spiritually, when we rise above a situation of action and intent, we are in a place of non-judgement and our understanding translates into compassion.

The absence of judgement leads to and makes available understanding of all things.

Understanding of any thing makes available compassion for that thing and dissolves the need for judgement.

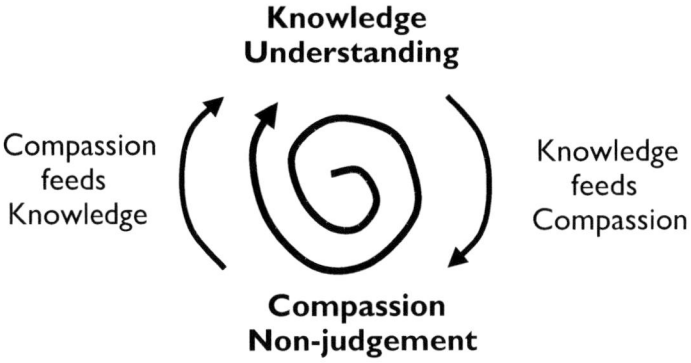

Figure 9: The Spiral of Knowledge and Compassion

As we dwell in the natural availability of compassion from knowing and non-judgement and the natural availability of knowing and non-judgement from compassion, we are reminded of the Zen Archer and our rediscovery of 'sin' and 'repentance'.

Understanding anything, including that we are off the mark, makes available compassion. This dissolves the need for judgement, naturally returning us to the mark. To quote from earlier in this book: "To get back on the mark, we must understand that we are off the mark in such a way as we naturally correct our misalignment with the mark and our target."

What does this have to do with understanding the Universe and ourselves?

When we are on the mark, when we have compassion, we have access to natural knowing.

Through continually staying on the mark, through compassion and non-judgement, we can naturally come to know ourselves and the mysteries of the

Universe. This is the beautiful, mystical spiral of spiritual growth, compassion and knowledge.

We grow spiritually, just as fallen rain seeps, trickles, cascades and gushes towards the sea.

From the moment when water from clouds falls as rain, the will of gravity draws it towards the sea. So it is with the Will that pulls us to grow spiritually through expanding our knowledge, understanding and compassion drawing us home towards the endless spiritual sea. Our spiritual growth is inevitable.

This is our soul journey. We can empower it by knowing our purpose, creating and living a vision. We can hear its call as we still our mind and listen to intuition. Forgiveness and love ease and accelerate the turning of the spiralling wheel of transformation.

As we grow with the mystical spiral of self-knowledge and compassion, we begin to recognise that it is the Will of the Universe that pulls us, like gravity towards the spiritual sea of Universal Knowledge. Through each of our journeys towards unending, unconditional love and compassion, we bring drops of knowledge to the Whole. As these drops of knowledge merge, interpenetrate and become one, rippling out into the sea, Universal self-awareness emerges. Each of us, all of us and none of us.

We have expanded from considering the contribution of each one of us into a vision of Universal self-awareness for all of us, but we can already feel that this is just one ripple in the rich textured sea. The same spiral of compassion and knowledge is at work in communities, organisations, governments, societies and our global community.

Part I: Purpose and Vision

Wherever there are aligned and connected groups of people, the spiral of compassion and knowledge is at work.

Communities, organisations and societies grow and learn. In this spiral of transformation, purpose may propel us, vision may draw us, suffering may drive us, but behind everything and always is the universal gravity, the Will of the Universe to know itself through us, expressed through the Emerging Global Transformation.

As we look out into the Self of the Universe, we look deep into our own Self. As we look inside our Self, we see the Self of the Universe.

In the words of a Native American saying: "If you seek to understand the whole universe you will understand little. If you seek to understand yourself you will understand the whole universe."

There are more ways of hearing, seeing, understanding and feeling the Emerging Global Transformation than there are human beings on our planet.

Wherever we see systems and structures for improvement and learning, the Emerging Global Transformation is at work.

Quality Management and Performance Management systems provide structures and processes for improvement and learning. I have observed the movement towards Quality Management and Performance Management by African, US, UK, Japanese and European civil servants and businesses large and small. The global quality movement, the European Foundation for Quality Management, EFQM Excellence Model, the Japan Quality Awards, the African Excellence Model and Malcolm Baldridge Awards in the US all demonstrate this

81

movement of change. The US Government Performance Results Act (GPRA) and the UK Government Best Value and Comprehensive Performance Assessment (CPA) legislation are part of the same global movement. Performance Management and quality management are examples of feedback and improvement systems working in organisations. The use in the military of the 'OODA Loop' of Observe-Orient-Decide-Act as a way of ensuring effective feedback and response is another example.

Performance management provides the structures and processes to allow large organisations and systems to improve and transform to play their part in global change.

Aligning Global Corporations with the Emerging Global Transformation: Global corporations are the engines of today's global economy. They have effective business performance management systems and the ability to implement policies globally. Through a small shift in policy, a global corporation can potentially make a massive difference to, for example: human health through changing what millions of people eat; the environment by changing what products get made; and human rights by changing working conditions.

It is a popular truism in business that "what gets measured gets managed and what gets managed gets done." Another popular statement is: "measurement drives behaviour". Changing what is measured and managed by a global corporation has the potential to change the behaviour of the corporation and its impact on our global system.

I am very optimistic about the potential to drive rapid change across large systems by a 'butterfly wing' change to performance management measures on which managers around the world are paid.

One simple insight offers us access to the gift of knowledge:

When we choose compassion, we deepen our intuition and receive the gift of knowledge.

To be powerful in influencing a system without the need for force, we must understand it. To understand it, we must have compassion for it. So long as we feel the need to judge, we are powerless. So long as we have enemies, we are weak. When we have compassion for our enemy, the dynamic is changed. We may still not promote their behaviour, but we are not trapped by losing our compassion and hence our understanding and power of insight and influence.

To be powerful in the face of our enemies, we must have compassion. This gives an insight into the practical biblical advice: "Love your enemy."

We can use our judgements and fixed opinions to point to our own weaknesses. Once we identify and correct a weakness in ourselves, we can understand and forgive it in others. When we forgive we have peace of mind. When we understand we have wisdom.

To explore and deepen your experience of knowing through compassion, try *Exercise 20. Knowing the unknowable* on page 149.

19. Emerging vision: parts of the whole

"Whatever you can do, or dream you can, begin it. Boldness has genius, power, and magic in it. Begin it now."

Goethe

South Africa Experience: In 2001, I was privileged to be a resource person to the Southern Africa Emerging Leaders Programme in Cape Town. One of the presentations was given by Mr Ncebe Facu, former Robin Island Prisoner for 13 Years and now the Mayor of the town formerly known as Port Elisabeth. Port Elisabeth is now a part of "Nelson Mandela Metro". Mayor Facu described how every day in Robbin Island prison, each of the prisoners attended classes for hours every day, learning, planning and preparing themselves for their vision of majority rule in South Africa. He pointed out how for many people, the peaceful transition of power that happened in South Africa was a miracle, but for them, it was exactly what they had envisioned, planned, trained for, expected and finally implemented.

To be effective in the world, we need both Vision and to be able to Implement or build our vision through planning and action.

We may dedicate our lives to personal success and financial gain, only to find that there is no satisfaction or security in what we have achieved. We may dedicate our lives to making a difference and serving others, only to find that we are without the resources to give our gift and make the difference of which we dream.

If we are to experience great success and sustainable satisfaction, we must find a way to serve. If we are to achieve great service by using the resources that come from material success, we must find a way to influence the way that resources are used.

Consider the statement that:

**If we want to experience real satisfaction from success, we need to make a difference.
If we want to make a difference, we need to be materially effective and successful.**

Individually, we are at a turning point, because in the wealthiest societies, we are realising that more money and more things do not deliver joy and satisfaction.

More power does not necessarily mean more security. More work and achievement in the old model will not give us a life we love or a future worth choosing.

20. Magnetic alignment

Our activities and intentions are like magnets. They can add to one another or cancel out. To be most strongly magnetic, a vision must meet our Physical, Emotional, Mental and Spiritual (PEMS) needs. The more that a vision meets all of our PEMS needs, the more sustainably it can satisfy us. As we noted in 19 above: If we want to experience real satisfaction from success, it helps to make a difference, (meeting a spiritual need.) If we want to make a difference, it helps to be materially effective and successful, (meeting a material need).

What makes a purpose and vision magnetic?

The more a vision meets all of our own needs, the more it will sustainably motivate us.

A vision may be attractive to one person, but not to another. For example, if one person's vision is to take the land of another, it is not magnetic to the person who would lose the land.

The more that a vision meets all of another person's needs, the more it will sustainably attract and magnetise *them*.

If our vision is based on fear it makes us a victim of that of which we are afraid.

If our vision is built on negative judgement of others, it is likely to alienate those whom we judge, or those whom we have not forgiven or for whom we do not have compassion.

To make a vision magnetic for a person, make it:
- win-win, not win-lose;
- based on love not fear or afflictive emotion;
- based on compassion, not judgement;
- meet personal PEMS needs.

To make a vision magnetic for others, make it:
- meet the needs of everyone involved;
- meet society's needs;
- meet humanity and the planet's needs.

Personal alignment and alignment with others

Each of us consciously or unconsciously tries to align our actions with our vision. When we align our vision and actions with our purpose and with the Will of the Universe, the power of the Universe flows through us.

When we have no purpose for our life, we may do many things and achieve very little, because our activities and intentions take us in different directions.

Each of the arrows in the diagrams below represents an intention or activity of a person. The box containing arrows represents the person. (You can also think of the box as a team, an organisation or a nation that is unaligned.)

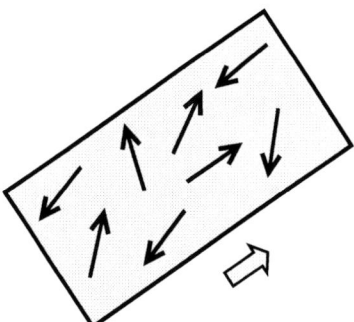

Figure 10: When we live without aligned purpose, we achieve little

When we find our purpose, it allows us to align the different parts of our lives. By aligning our lives with a purpose that meets all of our physical, emotional, mental and spiritual needs, we become more effective, successful and happy. When all of the activities in our life are aligned to our purpose, they fit together and have meaning.

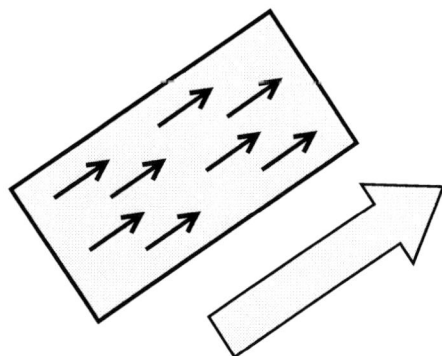

Figure 11: When we align with purpose we achieve more

We find it easier to change and adapt because we have a reason to change and adapt to follow our purpose.

When we are aligned with our purpose, we become magnetic to other people, to circumstances and to the things that we intend. This is a way of understanding how synchronicity works.

(The same also applies to a team, an organisation or a nation that is aligned: it is more effective, more able to change, more magnetic, attracting people organisations and circumstances.)

We can expand what is possible by expanding the resources that we have available by partnering and networking to achieve a shared vision.

If we partner with people who partner and network with people who network, there is no limit to the resources available to achieve a shared vision. When we partner, then we become a larger networked self.

Part 1: Purpose and Vision

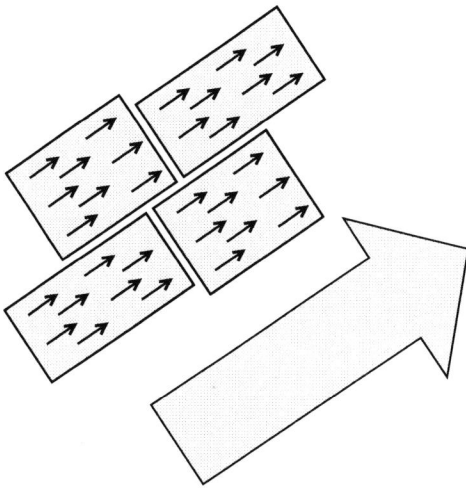

Figure 12: Aligned people are magnetically attracted to one another.

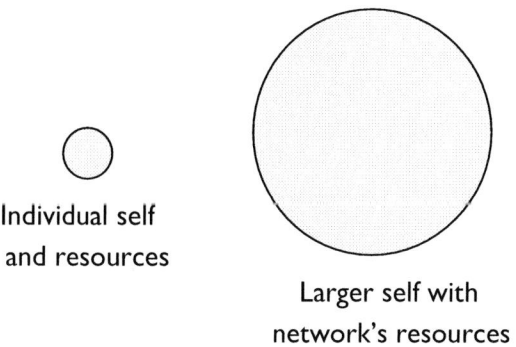

Individual self and resources

Larger self with network's resources

Figure 13: Networking to Build Resources

The more aligned resources and actions we can apply to our vision, the more capability we have and the bigger the impact.

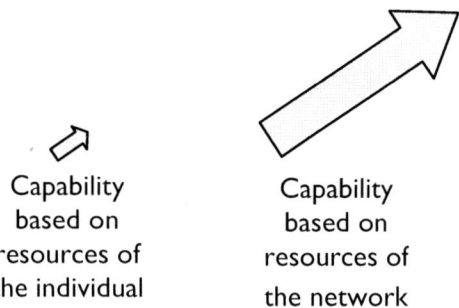

Capability based on resources of the individual

Capability based on resources of the network

Figure 14: Greater Capability of Aligned Resources

Aligned and magnetic people share resources and experience. They become more effective, produce more results and have more fun and are more successful.

The Emerging Global Transformation, the flow of change in the world, is magnetic too. Things happen because they fit with the Emerging Global Transformation.

Mandla Mentoor and the Soweto Mountain of Hope

In 2004, I am flying to Cape Town, South Africa from Johannesburg. I become aware of someone beside me. I look up from my papers and see a black South African moderately dressed. Although I have documents to review, I feel prompted to know more about this person. He has a special light, a charisma, a magnetism.

As I share, ask, listen and smile, I discover Mandla Mentoor. Mandla is on his way to an awards ceremony where he had been nominated as one of the top 3 social entrepreneurs in South Africa.

Mandla is naturally enlightened, naturally loving, naturally positive, and a natural leader. I prompt and listen to extraordinary stories of a life that has been lovingly, humbly and powerfully dedicated to service. For example: "People were saying that boys in Soweto were no good. I said they had nothing to do, so I organised a football league for the boys."

Another example: "There was a hill in Soweto that everyone used as a rubbish tip. I got the children to collect all the rubbish and sort it into piles. We then sold the sorted rubbish and used the money for the community. They also made things out of the rubbish. I wanted to show that there is economic value in waste".

My sense is that Mandla creates 'miracles' and magnetises people because of who he is.

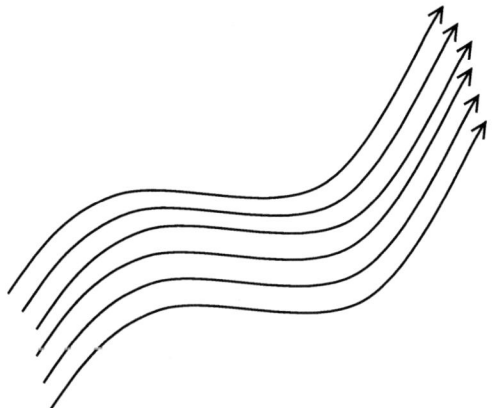

Figure 15: The Emerging Global Transformation has its own magnetic field

Aligned and magnetic people naturally align themselves with the Emerging Global Transformation. As a result, they are even more successful, because the wave of change drives their success rather than forcing them to change. Things happen without struggle, so life is more fun.

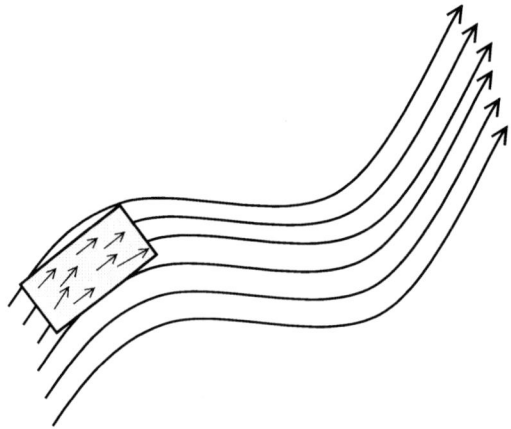

Figure 16: When we align with the Emerging Global Transformation the power of the Universe flows through us.

With the right resources and actions anything is possible. With the right actions, any resources can be acquired or at least shared through partnership. When we share a vision with another person, we create and own a shared future. When this future is aligned with each of our purposes then our shared vision benefits from each of our resources, each of our actions and the Universal power available to each of us in fulfilling our purpose.

When two or more of us align with a shared vision that furthers the Emerging Global Transformation, anything is possible. We become a channel, a portal and a conduit for Universal power. In more traditional language:

"For wherever two or more are gathered together in my name, there I am in the midst of them"

(Matt. 18:20).

When our vision is aligned with the magnetic pull of the Emerging Global Transformation we have potential partners everywhere.

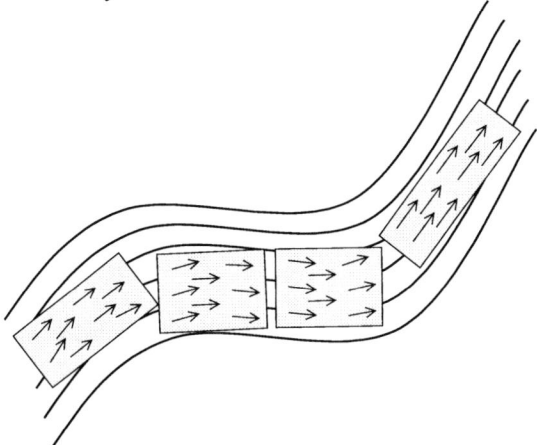

Figure 17: Partnering in Service of the Emerging Global Transformation.

When we partner in service of the Emerging Global Transformation, we are serving the purpose of all of humanity and all of the resources on the planet become available to us.

The same also applies to a team, an organisation or a nation that is aligned: it naturally aligns itself with local and global trends. Performance Management provides the structure and process for the alignment of purpose, vision and action across an organisation.

For sustainable success a person aligns with fulfilling their own Physical, Emotional, Mental and Spiritual needs and the needs of those around them.

For sustainable success an organisation aligns itself with fulfilling the needs of all of its stakeholders and so aligns their resources too.

Potentially governments and multinational organisations have access to immense power by aligning their purpose, vision and objectives with the needs of the Emerging Global Transformation.

Business Comment: To access the power of the Emerging Global Transformation for commercial success and making a difference, organisations need structure and process for alignment at every level. The structure and process for this alignment is being provided by the fusion of governance systems, quality management, performance management and knowledge management. The combination of maturity models like the Capability Maturity Model and the Plan-Do-Check-Act cycle of quality management can provide an engine for governments and organisations to align and drive transformation and so to play their part in the Emerging Global Transformation. See www.MindOfMany.com for links to related papers and documents.

How one person can change an organisation or community

An organisation is made up of networks of people. An aligned person is magnetic and can develop an aligned network of people around them, through example. Each person in an aligned network or team can stretch out their influence and build their own network of alignment. Alignment is magnetic. It spreads. This is how one person can change an organisation.

As alignment spreads across an organisation, the organisation itself becomes aligned and magnetic. By developing personal alignment of purpose, vision and action, a person can become magnetic, attract and align others, align with the change that is happening in our world and live a more effective, successful and happy life.

As we participate in relationships, families, communities, businesses and governments based on alignment of purpose, vision, actions and resources, our boldest, most daring vision becomes possible.

When we partner in service of the Emerging Global Transformation, we are serving the purpose of all of humanity and all of the resources on the planet become available to us. With these resources, anything is possible.

In our commitment to create a world worth choosing, we have partners everywhere that we have yet to meet.

It's up to us to find each other and work together.

Between us, we have significant resources of commitment, knowledge, experience, influence and wealth. If these resources act in alignment, they can change the course of history and create a new future for humanity.

It is up to us to make sure that our resources do act in alignment, but how can we communicate and share with others of like-mind and vision.

The Internet is here now, when we need it, to help us to share knowledge and ideas, to learn from one another in our transformation and to help us to collaborate in transforming our lives, our corporations, society, governments and our world. The Internet is a global tool for our global transformation. It is up to us to make sure that we use it that way.

As we form partnerships for transformation in an aligned global network, we become unstoppable.

As we choose to own the future, the world will never be the same again.

The future is yours. The future is ours. When we think, when we speak, when we spend, when we work, when we invest, we create the future. At this time, as never before we can say:

In a world ripe for transformation, one flap of my butterfly wing can change the world.

Think of your vision as a 'Castle in Your Mind'. See it, hear it, feel it, think about it.

As we imagine our highest vision, the Castle in Our Mind, it becomes real in our mind.

The reality in our mind magnetises the people and circumstances into our life to make our vision real.

As our life unfolds to build our highest vision, we come to know our true power and the greatest privilege of being alive.

Business Insight: We see the Emerging Global Transformation at work in the pressure on organisations to change and improve. The commitment of corporations and governments to learning and using best practice for quality management and performance management is like your and my commitment to personal development. Like a person, an organisation has consciousness. Just as our nervous system 'grounds' our consciousness as human beings, so the computer systems and communications networks of organisations provide a foundation for the consciousness and collective intelligence of teams, departments and organisations. Just as we are forced to transform by the challenges of change, so organisations are forced to transform by the challenges of change. Just as we can use vision, meaning and purpose in life to 'pull' our own personal transformation, in the same way, organisations can use vision, meaning and purpose to magnetise people in driving change. Just as we can discipline ourselves as human beings to still the mind, think clearly and learn from our experience, so organisations can adopt habits and disciplines to enable their collective intelligence and learning.

Just as we can become successful well-rounded people by learning to develop and grow, so organisations that put in place habits, disciplines and structures to support their ongoing transformation can achieve sustainable success.

The competitive pressure to achieve is forcing the evolution of organisations, corporations and governments. Just as we can see karma forcing each of us to individually develop and grow as a part of the Emerging Global Transformation, we can see karma operating on organisations to do the same.

Experience: City and Town Renaissance and purpose, vision and personal transformation

My experience in working with businesses and governments is that when people are motivated, inspired and lit up, extraordinary results can be produced. When they are not, projects move slowly or not at all.

There is a global movement to create communities, towns, cities, regions and nations which are beacons of human dignity and accomplishment. Since 2000, I have worked with teams in towns or networking cities and towns in Russia, UK and Africa.

With the shifting of economic activity and changes in political climate, whole regions can be left behind economically and lose their sense of purpose.

I have had the privilege to work with inspired and inspiring people supporting national or regional networks and working in individual small towns. Behind regeneration policies and programmes is the core question: "How can we stimulate a movement of self-propelling positive growth in a town, city or region?" There are recognised 'Critical Success Factors' for renaissance, urban renewal and regeneration. Depending on the country, millions or billions of Pounds, Euros, Dollars or Rands are being spent. Selections or 'baskets' of measures or Performance Indicators show where improvement is needed.

In the UK for example, 'Floor Targets' define minimum target levels for a community including, the age at death of men and women, the number of teenage pregnancies, and the education of 16 year olds. In South Africa, national measures show % of households with Free Basic Services of water, sanitation and electricity. Sophisticated policies define how a town or city should consult, involve citizens and develop its plan. In reviewing 'best practice' for development of communities, towns and cities 'attitudinal and cultural change' is recognised as a critical success factor.

Everywhere that I have worked I have seen individuals and teams who are making disproportionate difference to the lives of communities, or national programmes. People who are making the difference are the ones 'lit up' by a sense of purpose and vision which lights up others.

Community, city, national renaissance, comes down to people experiencing their lives, their potential differently and acting accordingly. When we are lit up with a sense of purpose and vision, we naturally create beautiful spaces and value-creating businesses.

Personal transformation and self-realisation costs nothing, but is the beginning and ending of community development, town, city and national renaissance. Anyone in regeneration and renewal can point to examples of huge amounts being spent with no real difference being made.

What would be the impact on outcomes (improving people's lives) if the majority of capital budgets were only released when purpose and vision are present?

Governments and societies continue to function with the level of personal motivation and engagement we have today. What could we achieve if we were inspired and lit up in our work? What could we achieve if a core role of 'human resources' was to support people in connecting with a personal sense of purpose and vision?

21. Why have a big vision?

Sometimes more is less! We think that if achieving something is difficult, then achieving something smaller will be easier. This is not always true. Sometimes we aim for a small vision, live with a small purpose in the hope that life will be easier.

With a small vision and a small purpose, there is not enough motivation to change, so we wait for suffering to force us to change.

To use a popular metaphor, if the vision, a tree in the picture below, is too small, then when an obstacle (a mountain) gets in the way, the vision is hidden from view of your eye.

A small vision is easy to see when there are no challenges. The tree can be seen from your eye.

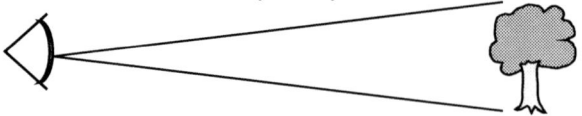

Figure 18: It is easy to see a vision when there are no obstacles

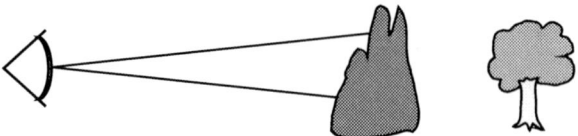

Figure 19: An obstacle hides a small vision

The mountain blocks the tree from sight.
A big vision is still visible even when obstacles appear.

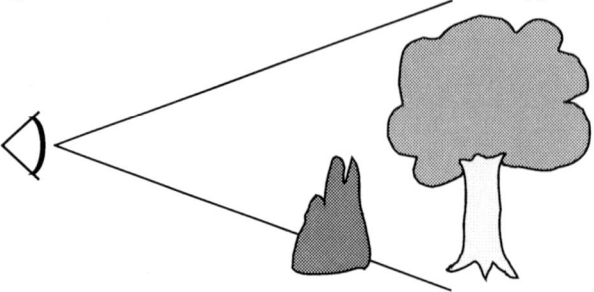

Figure 20: A big vision can be seen beyond the obstacle

The large tree can still be seen behind the mountain.

If your life feels too challenging, then why not create a bigger, more inspiring vision to motivate you?

Part 1: Purpose and Vision

The Old World

Building on the metaphor of the tree and mountain, for the most economically fortunate at least, the Old World was different with:

- stable economy
- long-term employment
- clear rules for success, based on a known path.

Our path in the Old World was easy to define:
Purpose = Be successful
Vision = Success within the system
The old landscape of success was a well-defined series of trees (visions) and mountain (challenges).

Figure 21: Old World – a well-defined series of challenges and opportunities

For example in the education and career system of the West the fortunate progressed by meeting a series of challenges.

Education		**Career**		**Success**	
Examination	Qualify	Interviews	Job	Promotion	Success

101

This was a motivator so long as we trusted society to provide for our material needs of security and we could expect a job and a good standard of living in return for all of the effort.

One problem comes when our employer or our society fails to provide a reward for success, then we need to be able to find our own way. When the stress of success becomes too much or material success is not enough to meet all of our physical, emotional, mental and spiritual needs, we have to find our own way.

In the Old World, in developed countries, the path seemed clear:
Education + Career = Success.
In the New World there is no simple rule.

The New World

The New World is different. Even in the richest, most privileged societies we are challenged by:
- uncertainties in global and national economies;
- shorter-term employment, often not guaranteed;
- increasing inequality: the rich get richer while poverty increases;
- new rules for success based on our ability to change and adapt.

Our path to success in the New World is different. The key to success is in our ability to transform ourselves.
Purpose = We have to discover it!
Vision = We have to create it!
The new landscape of success is trees (visions) and mountains (challenges) in all directions.

Part 1: Purpose and Vision

Figure 22: New World – challenges and opportunities everywhere

To find our own way we must find and live our purpose and choose and live our vision. Finding and living our purpose is both a challenge and a reward in itself. Finding and building our vision is both a challenge and a reward in itself.

Find Purpose   **Develop Vision**   **Change Myself**

Karma guides us to the vision (tree) that is right for us and defines the challenges (mountains) that we need to cross. We develop our intuition to choose how to cross the mountains. To quote from Chapter 16. *Karma: the gift of free tuition* on page 67:

Karma defines the mountains that we must cross to grow and develop spiritually.

This book provides simple tools to help us to find our purpose and vision and have the courage and tools for the journey across the mountains.

22. Vision, planning and affirmation exercises

"Never doubt a small group of thoughtful, committed people. They can change the world. In fact, nothing else ever has."

Margaret Mead

A perfectly created vision, reinforced in your mind through meditation, creates a force field that shapes reality.

Use the exercises introduced below to magnetise your vision into reality in our world.

| Create your vision | Exercise 21: The Castle In Your Mind: a Vision that makes a difference – p151. You can use this exercise to expand your vision of the difference you can make, by creating a vision for a project or for your life. Our lives are limited by what we believe to be possible. Our well-trained minds restrict us from thinking 'outside the box'. This helps us to stay focused, but it may not help us to find joy and satisfaction. |

Create affirmation cards for your vision	**Exercise 22: Creating Vision Cards** – p155. In this exercise, you create Vision Cards with affirmations that reflect the Castle In Your Mind. When you review these affirmations, they draw you into the future. When you review them daily, you become a magnet for your vision and your vision becomes your reality.
Creating a plan for your vision	**Exercise 23. Creating Your Vision Plan** – p159. Use this exercise to create a path, road map, flow diagram or flow chart to take you step by step to your vision. This exercise uses a simple, powerful approach that applies equally to grounding a personal vision, planning a family project, developing a breakthrough business plan or developing a plan for a community.
Creating a magnet for your vision through visualisation	**Exercise 24. Visualisation Practice** – p162. Find a regular time for this practice which you can do in anything from a few minutes, for example morning before getting up and each evening before sleep. Keep a pen and pad of paper beside you to capture any insights that you may have.

You can use these practices practised daily for 40 days to animate your life with new levels of vision and possibility.

Continue to use these practices and you will begin to notice the pattern of the Emerging Global Transformation as it touches your life with coincidences and miracles allowing you to live your purpose and shape our world.

23. You and I make the difference

In every moment, we shape our future. With a promise, we can reach into the future and change our destiny and our world. This book, Part 1 of The Book of Personal and Global Transformation, has taken us on a journey into our purpose and vision and out into our vision for the world. In this moment, we may see and feel the possibility of a New World. To make this seeing and feeling ever present in our lives we must be living into our vision.

Every day, we pass, like ships in the night, by extraordinary people of love, commitment and passion, not recognising one another in the throng of life.

To be partners in the Emerging Global Transformation, we must claim who we are and dare to shine in our world.

As we acknowledge and live our own magnificence, we allow others to do the same.

Or, as President Nelson Mandela quoted from Marianne Williamson in his inaugural speech:

"As we let our own light shine, we consciously give other people permission to do the same. As we are liberated from our fear, our presence automatically liberates others."

Marianne Williamson

Continuing, we can add:

At this extraordinary gateway moment, your light is precious, needed and celebrated, for as you dare to shine you light up others. And as ripples

of light pass around the world, day is breaking on a New World, your world and my world.

This is the world we have dared to dream of and now can build, together, in courage, in love, in celebration.

24. Summary of Part 1: Purpose and Vision

To play our fullest part in the Emerging Global Transformation and fulfil our destiny we develop and grow.

- **Purpose**: The greatest gift to ourselves and our world is to know and live our purpose.
- **Choice**: As we move beyond reaction and give up afflictive emotion, we have clarity of thinking and free will to choose.
- **Boundaries**: As we honour and develop our boundaries we maintain and develop our ability to manifest, to make our mark in the world.
- **Forgiveness**: When we forgive ourselves and others we gain peace of mind.
- **Intuition**: As we still the mind and listen, we have access to intuition.
- **Intentional**: We can enhance our power, by working with the power of intention, but with power comes responsibility.
- **Karma**: It is wise to respect karma if not by name then in being responsible for the consequences of the choices that we make.
- **Love**: When we act with love, we can work safely with the power of our own intention. Until we do this, any benevolent power would keep us from being powerful, to protect us from the damage we could do to ourselves by damaging others.
- **Surrender**: When we surrender to love the unseen world can accelerate our transformation and bring us to an experience of bliss.

- **Compassion**: Through compassion, we gain insight into the meaning inherent in a situation, rather than imposing our own meaning through judgement. Through boundless compassion, we have access to boundless insight, knowledge and understanding. Through compassion, we can gain insight into and knowledge of the unseen world from which reality unfolds.
- **Vision**: In our most daring vision, we each see part of the whole. Together we can emerge a shared vision for a New World.
- **Shine**: As we dare to shine the light of our love, we allow others to do the same and a new day breaks over our world.
- **Give**: By gift of karma and the extraordinary time at which we live, as we give from the love we receive, the love we receive is further magnified.

25. A gift received and offered

This book was a gift to me, given as a seed that has been nurtured and grown before it was offered on to you in love. It has been my teacher and my companion. The more love I have poured into it, the more blessings it has shone into my life.

If you have found this book valuable in kindling your own light, please give the same gift to others. You can download this book or buy printed copies from the website below.

This book is the first part of '**The Book of Personal and Global Transformation**' one butterfly wing contribution to the Emerging Global Transformation. If you would like to contribute to, refine, extend or facilitate transformation with the ideas in this book, please visit the website below.

www.MindOfMany.com

26. Guidelines for Exercises

I recommend working through the exercises sequentially. They build powerfully on one another in a way that I only discovered through personal experience doing the exercises.

Here are some suggestions for getting the most out of the exercises in the book.

Have fun

Because we think differently, more creatively when we are having fun.

With a life partner or business partner

These exercises help us to know ourselves and can help us to build understanding, empathy, compassion and support with a partner.

With a partner or a group

To develop common purpose and vision and share and support one another in the journey, learning from each person's insights.

Use a meditative state

Because when we enter a meditative state, our thoughts can delve into the unseen world and even shape the unseen world from which the seen world unfolds...

Bring sacredness to exercises, visualisations and meditations

Because bringing sacredness enhances the power of our intention. Intuition (and experimental evidence) suggests that prayers and intentions are more effective when accompanied by a ritual to bring sacredness, even though the religious framework from which the ritual comes does not seem to matter. As an example, try lighting a candle in a conscious and sacred way before starting and snubbing the candle on completion rather than blowing it out. Feel the difference.

Be conscious of diet and exercise

Because what we eat and the exercise we take affects the chemical and hormonal environment in our bodies affecting levels of endorphins (joy chemicals) in our bodies and seratonin (sometimes known as the God chemical, connected with spiritual experience). As an example, try a vigorous exercise set (subject to checking that your health is up to it) and experience the feeling of elation of endorphins during the exercise and when you have finished. As a further example, try the Kundalini Yoga set referenced on MindOfMany.com. Now imagine doing the same exercises the morning after an excess of alcohol…

Be conscious of the physical environment

Because a tidy, clutter-free, conscious, loved environment has a quality of sacredness. Feel the difference when you meditate in a physical environment that is conscious (tidy, purposeful, clutter-free) from one that is unconscious. As an example, try clearing anything that does not serve your purpose or vision from one room or area in your living space. Clean that area thoroughly and lovingly. If you can feel the difference, how about extending the clean-zone to every space for which you are responsible.

27. Exercise for Chapter 3: Purpose...

Life Change 1. Finding my purpose
Review the Guidelines for Exercises on page 111.

STEP 1. ✒Defining our terms✒
For each of the following words, list a series of words or phrases in turn which describe what it means to you:
Vision
Inspiration
Purpose

Take a few moments to explore these words and how they relate to one another. Write the three words as three points of a triangle on a page. Draw a picture or a diagram with arrows showing how you think that the different words support and are supported by one another.

Now check the definition of each if you have a dictionary to hand. What new insights does this exercise provide? What does purpose mean to you now?

One definition of purpose is:

My Purpose is my reason for being.

STEP 2. ✒List the high points of joy and satisfaction in your life✒
Now leave those definitions behind and let us delve into the pattern of your life. List the times of greatest satisfaction from your life. Just write a few words for each to describe what happened, or who did what. Brainstorm – just keep writing, one after another. Write down whatever comes to mind, even if it is embarrassing.

113

If nothing comes to mind, think of any moments of pleasure or satisfaction. When you run out of ideas, start from when you were born and try to remember a high point from each year. Go for volume, not for quality. If remembering some points makes you sad, just let that go. We'll work on that later.

Read the instructions above again and list any new ideas as they come.

STEP 3.   ✒Keep writing✒

You can spend anything from a few minutes to a couple of days in the process. Ten creative and focused minutes is fine.

Make the list a celebration of your life and of the things that have made it worthwhile and meaningful to you. Keep brainstorming until you have at least 20 points. Don't read on until you have. Try looking at nature, or things around you, to find hooks into new ideas, memories of joy, happiness, satisfaction or just good times.

STEP 4.   So what was the point of all that?

Well, as George Bernard Shaw said, "the true joy in life" is being "used by a purpose" which we recognise as "a mighty one".

When we are on purpose, we experience joy and satisfaction. By identifying points of satisfaction, we can see the pattern of purpose in our life and see where our satisfaction comes from.

The following diagram shows our path, moving one way and another as we pass through life.

Part I: Purpose and Vision

The moments when our path is aligned with our purpose, we experience the points of high satisfaction. The points of satisfaction are marked with 'X' in the diagrams below.

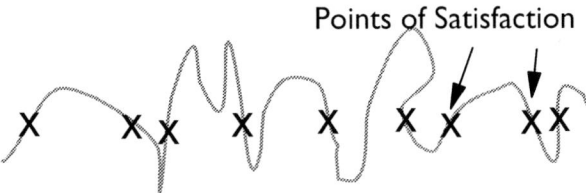

So, by finding those points of satisfaction, we can begin to uncover our purpose. Our purpose is the thread of meaning that we are touching when we experience these points of satisfaction. By looking for a pattern connecting these high points, we can begin to reveal our purpose. In the diagram below, our purpose is shown as a line connecting the points of satisfaction.

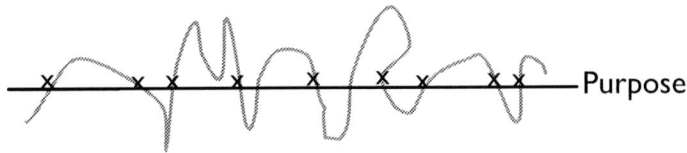

STEP 5. ✏ **Reflect on the thread of purpose** ✏

Reflect on your list, looking for the common themes, trying to group the different experiences inside these themes. What patterns do you notice?

Make a list of words, which captures the common themes. Speak each word, capturing the spirit of the word as you speak it. (For example, do not say excitement without being excited; don't say love without feeling love as you say it).

STEP 6. So who are you?

Now turn the string of words into a statement of purpose – a few words or a sentence. For example, you can express your purpose as a sentence by completing one of the following:

My purpose in life is:

✎ _____.

Because of who I am, because of my purpose, new futures are possible in the world.

I am the possibility of:

✎ _____.

When I live my purpose, I own the future. The future that I own is:

✎ _____.

Make a sentence starting with one of the expressions above and combining the common themes. Don't worry if it is an awkward sentence. Speak it out loud, capturing the spirit and meaning of the words as you speak them. If you can, speak your sentence to someone else. Ask them to let you know if you are not being your purpose as you speak it. If your voice is filled with the quality of, and inspired by, your purpose they'll score you 10/10. If your words are not spoken with commitment or excitement, then they will score you lower. The game is to learn to speak your purpose with more power, commitment and passion.

STEP 7. Yes, that is close to it, but what is the purpose behind that?

Refine your sentence. Simplify it. Be prepared to let some of the words go. What is the essence of your purpose? What is at the heart of your reason for being? Our purpose is profoundly beautiful, but often obscured by the challenges we have had in life – wrapped up for safekeeping. The real prize is not the wrapping paper, but what the wrapping paper contains. This image may be useful to get a sense of uncovering your purpose.

"The brown wrapping paper is crisp, clean and plain containing something. It holds great promise. Looking at it, my breath quickens. In this paper hides a gift of great importance.

Drawing back the paper reveals the gift – a beautiful perfect crystal. Now that I can hold and touch the beauty of the crystal, the paper has lost its appeal. The paper was to protect the crystal. The crystal is the prize."

The simple statement of your purpose is just the wrapper for your purpose. Your purpose is the real gift to you and your life and the gift of your life to the world. We protect the crystal in brown paper because it is special and sacred and to keep it safe for the right time. Now is the time. Imagine pulling back bunched brown paper to reveal the crystal. What is the beautiful crystal of your purpose?

STEP 8. Crystallise your purpose

Refine your purpose some more, or recreate it. It may not relate to what you have written down. What feels right? Try out different words. Does their sound inspire you? Imagine a vision of you living and fulfilling your purpose. What do you see? What purpose might you have which is so daring that you can hardly think, speak or write it, imagine or feel it? What purpose would fill your life with meaning and if fulfilled would validate and give meaning to your whole life, from birth to now and from now on? Try different statements of purpose. Write them down and speak them. Find the statement of purpose that feels right.

✎ _____.

Speak it now. Write it down. Or if nothing comes to mind, try to refine, to purify the sentence you created in STEP 5 and STEP 6 above.

If you did not need to struggle in any way to survive, what would your purpose be? If anything was possible to you, what would your purpose be? If twenty angels were gathered around you, working with you, helping you, so anything was possible, what would your purpose be?

✎ _____.

If everything in your life to date was preparing you for this moment of revelation, what would your purpose be? If the Universe had prepared you for a key role in the Emerging Global Transformation, what would your purpose be?

✎ _____.

Whatever purpose you have come to, you may always find that you can remove more brown paper or reveal an even more clear and beautiful crystal. You can always come back and do this exercise again to refine and clarify your purpose.

Practise speaking from your purpose and meaning what you say. Live and be what you say. Be on purpose as you speak your purpose.

You can develop your purpose over time. Purpose is your reason for being.

My reason for being is:

🖉 _____.

When we know our purpose, we know what resource, what raw material, what contribution we bring to the Emerging Global Transformation.

If you want to experience joy – live your purpose.

If you feel upset, sadness, anger, or frustration – correct your course and get back on purpose.

STEP 9. Sustainable joy – being an ambassador for purpose

Our purpose gives our life meaning only when we live it, not when we do not live it. Make a promise to live from your purpose. Write it down and put it in your wallet. Buy or create a piece of art that reflects or symbolises your purpose. If you use a computer, use your purpose in a screensaver. Build it into your habits and practices. (See Exercise 13 on page 155, Creating Vision Cards and Exercise 14 on page 162, Visualisation Practice.) Review it when you write a To Do List and relate what you are doing to your purpose. Express it through your work, your investments and your home. Be on purpose even when your children misbehave and you have had a hard day. Resolve always to be on purpose.

If you have found this exercise valuable:

Let the people around you – your partner, children and colleagues – know your purpose and ask them to support you in living from it. Be willing to stop whatever you are doing if someone points out that you are not living from your purpose. Take the time to communicate your purpose to your children so that they understand it. They are very good at seeing through inconsistency, so they are very good coaches!

If you want to be surrounded by joyful, satisfied people, support the people in your life to uncover their purpose and support them in living from purpose.

Make a list now of people in your life who might benefit from the same experience. If you are interested to share this exercise with others in your family, community, business, government or society, you can find materials to do so at: www.MindOfMany.com

28. Exercises for Chapter 6: Intuition...

Exercise 1.   A Simple Breath Meditation

Sit upright in a quiet place. It works best when the base of your spine is directly below your head and neck, so that your spine is about vertical.

Now close your eyes and breathe. Allow all of your attention to focus in a relaxed way on the rhythmic ebb and flow of your breath. If you find thoughts coming into your mind, let them pass by, like clouds across the sky. Experience the breath drawing from your belly, just below your navel. Allow your breathing pattern to change, so that the soft, rhythmic movement of your belly draws your breath in. As you do this, your ribs start to be moved less by the rise and fall of each breath. Continue this meditation for anything from 5 minutes to one hour.

The following works well for a short meditation:
1. **One minute of initial relaxation**
2. **Followed by twenty minutes of deep meditation**
3. **Two to three minutes of emerging mentally from the depths of the meditation.**

Always be gentle with yourself when you complete your meditation. Try not to jolt into action. Rather, return gently to normal awareness by breathing more consciously. Become aware of your body, for example by gently wiggling your toes and your fingers. When you are ready, quietly open your eyes and stay still as long as you need to before returning to normal daily activity. If you are disturbed during your meditation, try to resume and complete the meditation properly later.

Exercise 2. Breath Meditation: sinking deep infinite blackness

1. Relax, sit upright and breathe for one minute.
2. Then, for twenty minutes, with each out-breath, imagine your consciousness sinking into deeper and deeper meditation, descending into safe and infinitely deep blackness. With each in-breath do the same.
3. When you are ready to complete your meditation, allow each breath to bring you back towards consciousness, returning from where you have been.
4. After three minutes of normal breathing begin to wiggle your toes and fingers, then stretch and move your muscles and gently open your eyes when you feel you are ready.

Exercise 3. A Breath Meditation: transmitting and being charged with Universal Power

1. Relax, sit upright and breathe for one minute.
2. Now, imagine a glowing white or gold double helix of light feeding from above and spiralling down to touch the top of your head.
3. With each in-breath, imagine you are breathing in the helix of energy from the top of your head creating a glowing radiance around your body and energising you as it does.
4. With each out-breath, breathe out the spiral of energy through the base of your body and deep into the earth below you.
5. Experience yourself as a transmitter of energy and intelligence from the cosmos into the earth.
   - Experiment with breathing the spiral in from above and breathing out into your body's energy field or 'aura'. With each out-breath imagine and experience your aura growing and brightening. (I use this technique to raise my energy and to tap into spiritual power.)
   - Experiment with breathing the spiral rising from the earth on the in- breath and back to the earth on the out-breath.
   - Experiment with breathing the spiral from the earth on the in-breath and out through the top of your head to the heavens.
   - Do what feels right to the needs of your personal energy.
6. When you are ready to return to normal consciousness allow the intensity of the spiralling energies to subside.

7. Become aware of how your body has expanded energetically.
8. After three minutes of normal breathing begin to wiggle your toes and fingers, then stretch and move your muscles and gently open your eyes when you feel you are ready.

29. Exercises for Chapter 8: Free will...

Exercise 4.   I have a choice about REACTING with afflictive emotions

For this exercise, use one sheet of paper to list the items for question 1. Then, on subsequent sheets of paper, answer questions a) to c) for each of the items.

If you want to renew your life and be free of past anger, guilt, upset, and fear, spend time on this.

Look for places in your memory long forgotten. Be very honest with yourself. To help you to be more rigorous and determined, imagine that the future quality of your life, your parenthood, your contribution depends on it. Even if you have done exercises like this before, use this as an opportunity to go further and deeper, to leave you feeling more ready and enabled to live a life you love.

1. Has someone else or something else ever *made* me angry, guilty, upset or fearful? List examples, particularly the ones that still carry emotional charge for me.
2. For each of these, consider and write down the answer to the following questions:
    - a) What choice did I have in experiencing that emotion?
    - b) Did I have to get angry, guilty, upset or fearful?

- c) Who is responsible for the way I felt in each case?
3. Considering all the examples from question 1, who is responsible for how I feel now and in the future?
4. Considering all the examples from question 1, do I have the choice not to get angry or upset in future?
5. Are there any common themes or patterns that I can see from reviewing my reactions and actions?

Exercise 5. I have a choice about ACTING FROM afflictive emotions

1. Have I ever taken an action (including saying things) that resulted from anger, guilt, upset, or fear? List examples. Particularly note the ones where I caused harm that I regret or am ashamed of.
   For each example:
   a) What was the positive or negative impact for me?
   b) What was the positive or negative impact for others?
   c) Mark any of these examples that remain incomplete, unfinished, or about which I still feel an emotional charge (where there is still anger, guilt, hurt, upset or blame).
   d) In each case, what would have been the cost or benefit of waiting until I could act without the influence of anger, guilt upset or fear?
2. If I had a choice in the matter, would I choose not to act out of anger, guilt, upset or fear?
3. How can I reduce the damage I do when I am feeling angry, guilty, upset or fearful?
4. How can I reduce the length of time for which I stay feeling angry, guilty, upset or fearful?

When we ask questions like these, we stir up the submerged emotions that are stealing away our peace of mind and free will. When they are stirred up, it is a good time to wash them away!

To be ready to wash away these old emotions:
a. Make a list of those examples that still carry emotional charge. The fact that they carry charge indicates that they are still incomplete.
b. If you can see any actions that you could now take to 'clean up' or 'complete' any of the issues, include these in your list.

Exercise 6.   Seeing afflictive emotions at work

1. Can you see afflictive emotion playing a role in any of the following situations?
    - Bullying
    - Parental violence
    - Racial violence
    - Business decisions and strategy
    - Industrial relations
    - Political debate
    - International politics
    - War
    - War crimes

2. What do you feel or think about the following statements?
   "When I am angry, I always get it off my chest."
   "I always speak my mind."
   "They deserved what they got."
   "We will annihilate the competition."

3. What insight do these questions give you about the role of afflictive emotions in our world?

Exercise 7. Using Emotional Freedom Technique to be free of Afflictive Emotions

Say there is a topic of conversation, a memory that always makes you burn with righteous anger, red-faced and ready to punish the person concerned. You seem to have no choice. The topic comes up and you get angry. On a scale of 0 to 10, your anger is at 9 out of 10.

Or you have a memory which brings a feeling of deep guilt. You have had it for years, but even though you know it serves no purpose, you can't let it go. On a scale of 0 to 10, the guilt is an 8 out of 10.

Or every time you think of the dentist you feel sick with fear. The fear is 9 out of 10.

Using Emotional Freedom Technique (EFT), you can reduce the intensity of the anger or guilt or fear to a 4 out of 10 or a 2 out of 10 within a few minutes. Next time the situation arises, it no longer has the same hold on you. You still have the memory, but it doesn't trigger the intense emotion.

EFT is very simple. It is a part of a movement of emotional self-management techniques involving tapping. The website for this book has links to free self-study courses in EFT. EFT may not replace the personal change that comes from deep introspection, but it can be used to clear the debris of afflictive emotion to allow clear thinking and appropriate actions.

Brief EFT instructions are included here courtesy of Gwyneth Moss, an EFT instructor. It is worth taking a one-day course in EFT, or at least having someone show you how to do EFT the first time.
1. Identify an issue about which you immediately feel strong upset, anger, fear or guilt. Rate the intensity of the emotion on a scale of 0 to 10.
2. Follow the steps ABC below.
3. Rate the intensity again as described below.
4. You can repeat these steps and observe how the intensity of the issue subsides.

The diagram below shows each of the places to tap or rub, including the 'tender place' which you will need to find by experiment. There are also further EFT links on the web site WWW.MindOfMany.COM.

ABC summary of Emotional Freedom Technique

Awareness: What is the issue and what is the afflictive emotion? What tension, pain, memory or craving do you have. Name it. Be specific and detailed. How do you feel? What is the intensity on a scale of 0 to 10?

Balancing: Say three times as you gently massage the tender place…. "Even though I have this…(describe the problem)…..I truly and deeply accept myself"

Clearing: Tap with two fingers on each of the eight acupressure points starting with number 1, saying a few reminder words to keep the problem in mind. Tap the crown of your head last with all finger tips.

Now….Take a deep breath and close your eyes for a moment. Tune into the problem. Notice what has changed or what emerges. Measure the intensity again and repeat ABC on the remainder of the problem or on another aspect of the problem.

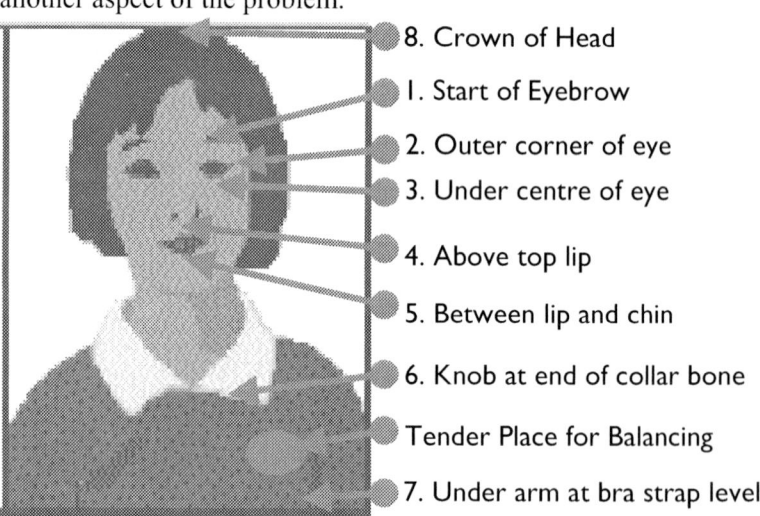

8. Crown of Head
1. Start of Eyebrow
2. Outer corner of eye
3. Under centre of eye
4. Above top lip
5. Between lip and chin
6. Knob at end of collar bone
Tender Place for Balancing
7. Under arm at bra strap level

Summary by Gwynneth Moss, from www.TrancePennine.co.uk

30. Exercises for Chapter 9: Radiating love

Life Change 2. Communicating with the heart

This exercise is based on the Freeze-Framer® technique described in Chapter 17. *Surrendering to love* on page 75.
1. Relax and be comfortable.
2. Become aware of your heart in the upper left-hand side of your chest.
3. With each in-breath, imagine that you are breathing into the heart.
4. With each out-breath, imagine that you are breathing out love from the solar plexus, where the ribs meet at the centre of the chest.
5. Think of someone or an animal that you unconditionally love and imagine that you are radiating love to them from the centre of your chest.
6. Notice how the vibration of your body changes as you continue to do this exercise. Bring your whole body to a vibration of love.
7. Practise radiating love to people and situations where you have felt afflictive emotions and observe the effect.
8. Practise radiating love into conversations and meetings and observe the effect.
9. Practise consciously radiating love when you hug a loved-one.
10. Develop the ability to bring a vibration of love to your whole body and surroundings.

31. Exercises for Chapter 11: Learning

Exercise 8. ༀ Reflect on forgiveness and boundaries ༀ

Meditate and reflect on the following:
- Are there situations where you are Powerless, Resentful or Angry *and at the same time* Happy & Effective?
- How do you balance forgiveness and boundaries?
- How do you behave at work?
- How do you behave as a parent?
- How would you like to behave?
- How might your life be different if you were always strong in both forgiveness and maintaining boundaries?
- How would you rate Mahatma Ghandi on forgiveness and boundaries?
- How would you rate Nelson Mandela on forgiveness and boundaries?
- How can we forgive, without giving up our power to a person who has wronged us?

Exercise 9. Giving up afflictive emotion by choosing compassion

The following suggestions and questions are useful for looking inside to find out whether afflictive emotion is due to a boundary that needs reinforcing or an old wound that needs healing.
1. Realise that the anger, guilt, upset or fear is inside you.

2. Did the person happen across some debris in your garden? Did they touch an old wound?
If so:
3. Understand the debris – what incident in the past was like the incident that just happened?
4. What unspoken anger, guilt, upset or fear did this incident cause to surface?
5. What actually happened that resulted in your getting upset? What were the actual events as opposed to your interpretation of events?
6. What meaning did you give to what happened?
This is the same as asking: "What judgement did you make about what happened?"
7. What different meaning could you give to what happened that would make you feel compassion for the perpetrator? For example, they had a bad day, or they have a difficult life.
8. Experiment with this and other alternative meanings and realise that your anger is a result of the meaning you gave to the event, not just the event itself.
9. Keep experimenting with alternate meanings including positive ones, sad ones and funny ones. Repeat this until you find that you can be detached from your original meaning.

As you recognise the meaning that you gave to what happened, you begin to recognise the debris in your garden. For example, if someone has 'made you feel' inferior, is it a pattern you have from the past? Can anyone ever make us feel anything emotionally, or do we have a choice?

10. Can you find a meaning where the event is blessing you, helping you to learn and grow, for example by pointing out where you need to create and maintain your boundaries?

Once you have recognised the debris, you can choose to remove it by choosing a meaning based on compassion, rather than judgement.

32. Exercises for Chapter 12: Forgiveness

The key Exercise for this chapter is the Forgiveness Spring Clean. As a part of your spring clean, you may use some of the other Forgiveness Exercises. Briefly review the following Exercises, before starting *Life Change 3. Forgiveness spring-clean* on page 138.

Exercise 10. Forgiving through Grace

It is possible to transform or forgive in an instant. Whether this is evidence of God, Universal power, or the power of heartfelt, honest human intention is unimportant. Before accepting years of pain or working through long exercises, we can use meditation and heartfelt intention to develop forgiveness.

The following simple steps can be used to forgive. If you are comfortable with prayer, then these steps can be combined with prayer.

1. Rate the intensity of the issue to be forgiven on a scale of 0 to 10.
2. Create a feeling of sacredness, humility and reverence. For example, meditate, be silent and light a candle.
3. Use one of the meditation practices described above to still your mind and find a place of spiritual power.
4. Create an honest desire to be rid of the pain that the un-forgiven issue causes.
5. Become aware of or imagine a benevolent Universal power or God.
6. Be aware of the thoughts, images and feelings relating to what must be forgiven.

7. Offer the issue to be forgiven to the benevolent Universal power or to God. Do this:
   - by speaking words asking the power or grace to forgive;
   - by creating an image of the person or situation disappearing into a point of divine light in the distance;
   - by sensing the pain draining from your body and being absorbed by Universal power and into the point of divine light; and
   - by realising that there is no point in carrying pain any longer.
8. Continue giving up and forgiving until you feel a sense of lightness.
9. Leave the issue in the hands of the Universal power.
10. Return from the meditative state.
11. Rate the intensity of the issue on a scale of 0 to 10 now.

Exercise 11. Forgiving a lifelong issue by writing and burning a letter

You can use this exercise to forgive someone who is not easy to contact or communicate with or someone who is deceased.

1. Create a sacred feeling, meditate and light a candle.
2. Be clear that your intention is to fully and finally be rid of the issue.
3. Write the communication as a letter, with all of the blame and anger expressed. Drain your negative emotions into the paper through your pen. Once you have vented the anger and blame, aim to take responsibility for the situation. When you are ready to, end your letter with a sentence to the effect that: "Having communicated all of this to you, I forgive you fully and finally."

4. In the sacred space that you have created, BURN THE LETTER or destroy it, rather than sending it. You are symbolically giving up and letting go of your perception and the afflictive emotions involved.
5. If you do this with the intention to let go of the afflictive emotions and to make way for the positive emotion, you may well find that what is left is an experience of compassion or love. While bathed in that experience, you are much more likely to be able to heal any external damaged boundaries that may still remain between you and another person.

Exercise 12.   Letting go of guilt: forgiving myself

Blame is often the automatic, unchosen, reaction when someone is 'off the mark', or perceived to be off the mark. Guilt is the result of blame applied to myself. I am guilty because I think I have done wrong; I am off the mark. Guilt is no fun. Do not let go of guilt simply to give up responsibility for past and present actions. Let go of guilt so that you can focus attention on getting back 'on the mark' and getting back on purpose.

The following insights, questions and affirmations may be useful in mastering guilt:
1. Does it support my purpose more to feel guilty about being off the mark, or to get back on the mark and stay there?
2. Be ruthless with guilt and compassionate with yourself. Remind yourself that guilt is just a way of avoiding taking responsibility, postponing the moment when we reclaim our free will and start to create a future worth choosing, by getting back on the mark.
3. People are not bad, just their behaviour. How do you need to change your behaviour so that you do not behave badly in future? What promise can you make to yourself or others so that you can forgive yourself

and move on? Try an affirmation like: "I have done something of which I am not proud. I promise to do my best to never make the same mistake again. I forgive myself, so that I can meet the challenges which my actions have created and so that I can focus on never causing these problems again."
4. Imagine yourself as an innocent child who has made a mistake. Be compassionate with the child. Imagine taking them (yourself) in your arms and saying.
"I forgive you and I'll help you to do it right in future."
5. We all have the ability to give up guilt. We just need to practise. Make a point of practising whenever you have the opportunity.
6. Do what you need to do so as not to make the same mistake again.
7. Challenge yourself to see how quickly you can give up guilt whenever you notice it.
8. Celebrate whenever you give up guilt and work on reducing the time it takes!

Exercise 13. Letting go of anger: forgiving others

Anger is an attempt to make someone or something, (for example a person, the Universe, or God), feel guilty. Anger is no fun. Do not let go of anger to condone wrongdoing. Let go of anger so that you can be most useful in correcting wrongdoing. Being off the mark (angry) does not help to make up for someone else being off the mark.

The following questions, insights and affirmations may be useful in mastering anger:
1. Does it support my purpose more to feel and express this anger about someone else or something else being off the mark, or to get back on the mark myself and stay there?

2. The more righteous the anger feels, the more off the mark your actions are likely to be when you express the anger. Be ruthless with anger and compassionate with the person you were angry with. Remind yourself that anger is just a way of trying to make someone else feel guilty. Will it really improve the situation if they do feel guilty? Anger is just a way of postponing the moment when we finally reclaim our free will and start to create a future worth choosing by getting back on the mark.
3. People are not bad, just their behaviour. How do you need them to change their behaviour so that they do not behave badly in future? What promise do you require them to make to you or others so that you can forgive them and move on? Try asking the question: "I am angry with X because they have done, said or thought something for which I want them to feel guilty. I forgive them and give up all desire to punish them, so that I can play my most constructive part in meeting the challenges which their actions have caused, rather than becoming a part of the problem myself."
4. Imagine the person or thing you are angry with as an innocent child who has made a mistake. Be compassionate with the child. Imagine taking the child in your arms and saying, "I forgive you and I'll help you to do it right in future."
5. We all have the ability to give up anger and stay on the mark. We just need to practise. Make a point of practising whenever you have the opportunity.
6. Challenge yourself to see how quickly you can give up anger whenever you notice it.
7. Celebrate whenever you give up anger and work on reducing the time it takes!

Exercise 14. Simply forgiving an innocent child

Visualise the person who you are angry with as an innocent child. Bring the issue you are angry about to mind and say or imagine saying to that person the words:
"I forgive you."
Keep communicating with your image of the person until you feel that you have forgiven them. Hear, feel and see the child say:
"I accept your forgiveness."
When you feel that you have forgiven the innocent child, embrace and thank them.

Exercise 15. Giving up guilt as an innocent child

Visualise yourself as an innocent child. Bring the issue you are guilty about to mind and say or imagine saying to yourself as a child:
"I forgive you."
Keep communicating with the image of yourself as a child until you feel that you have forgiven yourself. Hear, feel and see the child say:
"I accept your forgiveness and I give up my guilt."
When you feel that you have forgiven the innocent child, embrace and thank them.

Exercise 16. Reclaiming peace of mind

Meditation and silence build our resilience to difficult circumstances.

Anger, guilt, upset and fear steal peace of mind.

In addition to the deep peace that comes from consistent, regular meditation, the following insights, questions and affirmations may be useful in regaining peace of mind when we are disturbed by afflictive emotions:

1. Does it support my peace of mind to remain angry, guilty, upset or fearful?
2. Try the affirmation: "Peace of mind is important to me. I give up my right to be angry and to punish, so as to reclaim my right to peace of mind. From peace of mind I can see what is needed to resolve the problem, rather than being a part of the problem."
3. We all have the ability to regain our peace of mind. We just need to practise. Make a point of practising whenever you have the opportunity.
4. Challenge yourself to see how quickly you can regain your peace of mind whenever you notice you've lost your peace of mind.
5. Celebrate whenever you regain your peace of mind and work on reducing the time it takes!

Life Change 3. Forgiveness spring-clean

Spring-cleaning takes time and makes a big difference. Set aside several hours or a day for this exercise to get the most from it. Do it alone, with a coach or a friend.
There are many ways to forgive. Several exercises are provided above. They are a resource. Review these exercises as possible approaches to forgiveness. Use the ones that feel right for you. This Life Change provides a structure for a forgiveness 'spring-clean' – cleaning out anger and guilt from your life to be free and happy in the present and future. People with nothing to forgive have natural energy, positivity, magnetism and love of life. Forgiveness is worth it!

STEP 1. ✒ Write the definition of "TO FORGIVE" on a clean page. ✒

TO FORGIVE: To give up all resentment against, all desire to punish, to give as before...

🕊Reflect and meditate on the following questions. 🕊
Write down the immediate answers you receive on reading the questions.
How different would your life be if you had nothing to forgive?
What guilt could you give up, what one or two issues could you forgive that would change your life for ever?
In this exercise, decide to be courageous and focus on the life-changing issues.

STEP 2.   ✒Brainstorm issues to forgive. ✒

Focus on the issues that really matter to you. Focus on the places where forgiveness will change your life for ever. List every issue you can think of. Be very thorough. You can come back and work on other issues later. Make a page like the one shown on the following page.

Fill in Column 1: ISSUE with issues to forgive, by writing, for example:

I am angry with X to make them feel guilty for...
I am making myself feel guilty for....

Try to put all of the emotion you feel into the paper. Imagine the pain and negative emotion draining through your pen and into the paper.

You will use this list in a forgiveness ritual. As you are writing the issue, imagine that you are already forgiving. Smile. Sigh. Feel the tension lifting away. Think of the freedom of having forgiven. Notice any emotions or feelings as you do this.

BRAINSTORM: ISSUES TO FORGIVE	
ISSUE	DONE
I am making myself feel guilty for driving Mary away.	✓
I am angry with Mary to make her feel guilty for leaving.	
I am angry and upset with my mother who died before I was born ...	

STEP 3. Forgiving each item to be forgiven now

Review each item on the list:
For each item on the list, first try the simple exercise of forgiving them as an innocent child. If this doesn't achieve complete forgiveness, you can then choose to use another forgiveness approach later.

Visualise the person who you are want to forgive as an innocent child. Bring the issue you want to forgive to mind and say or imagine saying to that person the words: **"I forgive you."**
Keep communicating with your image of the person until you feel that you have forgiven them. Hear, feel and see the child say:
"I accept your forgiveness."
When you feel that you have forgiven the innocent child, embrace and thank them.
In some cases, you will find that this exercise is very liberating. Put a check mark in the **DONE** column for each issue completed.

If you find that they do not accept the forgiveness, or that you cannot give it, or that you cannot embrace them, do not put a check mark in the **DONE** column. We'll come back to these later.

For each item on the list where you are giving up guilt: Visualise yourself as an innocent child. Bring the issue you are guilty about to mind and say or imagine saying to yourself as a child:
"I forgive you."
Keep communicating with the image of yourself as a child until you feel that you have forgiven yourself. Hear, feel and see the child say:
"I accept your forgiveness and I give up my guilt."
When you feel that you have forgiven the innocent child, embrace and thank them.
Again, if this simple exercise brings a sense of peace and forgiveness, place a check mark in the **DONE** column of your list. You may find that this works for just a few, or nearly all of the issues to be forgiven.

STEP 4. Using other forgiveness approaches

Copy each of the issues that you did not mark as **DONE**, onto another piece of paper. When you have completed the burning ritual below, you can use one of the other forgiveness exercises for each of the incomplete issues. Use the one that feels intuitively right to you in each case. **Don't forget to make this separate list of issues to forgive using other approaches before you burn the original list!**

FORGIVE USING OTHER APPROACHES		
ISSUE	DONE	FORGIVE HOW?

I am angry with Mary to make her feel guilty for leaving.	Forgive through grace
I am angry and upset with my mother who died before I was born ...	Write and burn a letter

STEP 5. Declaring forgiveness

When you have visualised forgiving each item on the list, fold the paper and write on the outside:

"I forgive each of these people for all of the things for which I have wanted them to feel guilty as I would forgive an innocent child."

And:

"I forgive myself each of these things for which I have felt guilty as I would forgive an innocent child."

You are making a promise as you write this. It's a light but serious business.

STEP 6. Destroying the list by burning or tearing

Now take the paper outdoors, or to a fireplace and prepare to burn it. (If you can't burn it, have an envelope ready, so that you can tear the list into small pieces and place the pieces into the envelope). As you burn it or tear up the paper, say something to the effect of:

"As I burn (or tear up) this paper, I gladly give up all of my guilt and all of my anger so that I can live my purpose, reclaim my free will and be part of the solution, rather than part of the problem."

(If you feel comfortable with the words, you can also experiment with saying one or all of the following. Be open-minded and see what feels right for you.)

> "I ask my subconscious mind to assist me in forgiving, giving up and letting go."
>
> "I ask the Universe to assist me in forgiving, giving up and letting go."
>
> "I ask the angels to assist me in forgiving, giving up and letting go."
>
> "I ask God to assist me in forgiving, giving up and letting go."

Now say thank you and declare it done!

> "Thank you. So it is. So it is. So it is. It is done. It is done. It is done."

All of this puts your seal on your forgiveness.

If you burned the paper, ideally, scatter the ashes in a flower garden, park or river. (If you tore up the paper, sweep all the pieces into the envelope and deposit the envelope in a trashcan that is not in your home or office). However you dispose of the debris, smile when you do it.

STEP 7. Wash your hands

Finally, wash your hands to symbolically wash away the last remnants of what you have given up and let go. Reward yourself with a shower or a bath and imagine washing away all the debris of past guilt and anger. If you are going to take a bath, put a handful of salt into the water. It will help to make you feel all the cleaner.

If you feel sad, or emotional, that is fine. Just let the emotions pass through you. Observe them, do not become attached to them.

You can use this Life Change again – think of it like regular cleaning. Every time you clean, everything gets a little bit cleaner.

33. Exercises for Chapter 16: Karma

Exercise 17. Recognising karma

Use pen and paper to do the following exercise. You can use this exercise to draw out insights from past challenges. We will use the results in subsequent exercises to deepen our understanding of karma, compassion, insight, intuition and surrendering to love.
1. Consider a major challenge from your past that you now feel you have completed positively and moved on from.
2. Can you see that the same or a similar challenge has occurred at other times in your life?
3. What did the challenge force you to recognise or do and what have you learned from that recognition or action?
4. As a result of meeting and moving on from this challenge are you now more able to:
   - live your purpose;
   - be more courageous when faced by similar challenges;
   - establish clear and healthy boundaries in relationships;
   - forgive others for a weakness that you demonstrated when meeting this challenge;
   - be compassionate and understanding to others who suffer similar circumstances to those that you suffered;

- give love to others who experience a similar challenge;
- or accept that you are more authentically powerful than you previously knew?

5. Can you now see any way in which the challenge was a blessing to you? List ways in which the meeting and moving on from this challenge has been a blessing to you in becoming a more:
   - purposeful,
   - authentically powerful,
   - forgiving,
   - compassionate and
   - loving human being?
6. If we understand karma to be 'the relentless gravity that pulls us back to the mark' that is towards living our purpose with power, forgiveness compassion and love. Can you now recognise the action of karma in your life?
7. **Repeat:** Try steps 1-7 for other challenges that you have positively moved on from, until you can clearly see that challenges throughout your life have acted to bring you to the mark of purpose, power, forgiveness, compassion and love.

Exercise 18. Learning from karma

If karma is at work in our challenges, then by recognising and understanding what karma is offering to teach us, we can move on more rapidly from any challenge.

1. Consider a major challenge in your life today.
2. Can you identify that the same or a similar challenge has occurred at other times in your life?
3. Think deeply on the question: What is the challenge asking you to recognise, change in yourself, or do?

4. How would you have to grow and who would you have to become to make the recognition, change or take the action? What would you have to learn?
5. If you learned this, would you be more able to:
   - live your purpose;
   - be more courageous when faced by similar challenges;
   - establish clear and healthy boundaries in relationships;
   - forgive others for a weakness that you demonstrated when meeting this challenge;
   - be compassionate and understanding to others who suffer similar circumstances to those that you suffered;
   - give love to others who experience a similar challenge;
   - or accept that you are more authentically powerful than you previously knew?
6. Can you now see any way in which the challenge is a blessing to you in becoming a more
   - purposeful,
   - authentically powerful,
   - forgiving,
   - compassionate and
   - loving human being?
7. If you can answer: "yes" to any of the above, can you now recognise the action of karma in your life?
8. If you can see karma at work, you now have a simple choice: learn the easy way by learning the lesson, making the change, or learn the hard way by ignoring the lesson and waiting for karma to relentlessly force the challenge onto you again.

Recommendation: If you apply these questions to the challenges you face for a month it will become a habit.

You will begin to use your understanding of karma in decision making as a habit. As we do this, we become partners with the Universe in our own growth and transformation, recognising challenges as opportunities for insight and growth.

34. Exercises for Chapter 17: Love

Exercise 19. ꙳Surrendering to love: the easiest way to learn life's lessons ꙳

For this exercise, refer back to the challenges that you identified in the Exercises on 'Recognising karma' and 'Learning from karma'.

Surrendering to love is very simple and powerful, but not always easy. When we learn to make it a habit, we can live with great power and in an experience of bliss. We can live in 'Internal Heaven. In this exercise we intentionally surrender to love to dissolve afflictive emotion.

You will need a pad of paper and a pen.
1. Find a quiet place and a time when you can think and be uninterrupted.
2. Reviewing each of the challenges that you faced and learned from in the past (listed in Exercise 17 **Recognising karma** on page 144) can you see how the challenge has given you the opportunity to dissolve fear, anger, guilt and other afflictive emotions to become more loving?
3. Look inside yourself at your current emotions. Recognise any anger, fear, upset, guilt or stress that you are feeling.
4. Name each afflictive emotion and describe it, when it came about and how it came about. Are you familiar

with it? Have you experienced the same thing before? Do not blame anyone or anything for it, just describe what it is and how it feels.
5. Now say the following, or something like it. "I recognise this suffering. I have described it. I have had enough of it and I am willing to learn my lesson the easy way. I surrender my suffering to Love. I surrender my opinions, my beliefs, my emotions and my desires. I surrender it all to Love. I invite Love to wash me of my suffering and dissolve anything that it is not love. I surrender my power and control to the power and control of Love. I surrender my pride to the nobility of Love. I ask to see through the eyes of Love, to hear with the ears of Love, to think with the mind of Love and to feel with the heart of Love. I give up all of me that is not Love." You will know that you have successfully surrendered, because the heaviness, the attachment, the emotional suffering lifts away.
6. When you have surrendered, look for new insights into how to proceed. Be willing to change anything and everything. If you change your life through choice, the 'relentless gravity' of karma will not have to force change on you.
7. When you find yourself getting caught up in an afflictive emotion again, get into the habit of surrendering again.

35. Exercises for Chapter 18: Compassion

Exercise 20. Knowing the unknowable

1. Consider a person or situation that you judged or did not understand in the past, but you now understand and now respect without negative judgement.
2. Did you have any fixed opinions of the person or situation that you have since let go of?
3. How does understanding the person or situation help you to let go of the fixed opinion or judgement?
4. How does letting go of the fixed opinion or judgement help you to understand the person or situation?
5. In your personal experience, do fixed opinions and judgements make it harder or easier to be compassionate?
6. In your personal experience, does letting go of fixed opinions and judgements make it harder or easier to understand and know?
7. Repeat these steps considering different situations that you have found it hard to understand in the past, but understand today until you see a clear relationship between judgement and your ability to understand a situation.

It is easier to see in hindsight that absence of judgement helps us to understand a situation. Now try applying the same insight to current opinions and judgements.

Now consider something or someone in your life today that you find it hard to understand.
1. List any opinions or judgements that you have about that person or situation.
2. For each of the listed opinions and judgements, list three other possible opinions: one ridiculous (but

possible), one compassionate and one that shows that karma is at work in your life. For example if your opinion is: "She is a bad person." You might list:
Ridiculous – "She is a secret agent and has to do this to keep people at a distance."
Compassionate: "She made a mistake. She does her best."
Karmic: "She is there to help me to learn to live my purpose and grow to be loving and powerful. This is not the first time I have experienced a situation like this. I attracted this situation to learn a lesson – about preserving my boundaries or living my purpose."

3. Review these three possible opinions and realise that any one of them could be correct.
4. Now consider which of the three possible opinions leaves you more free from afflictive emotion, more able to follow your purpose and more able to understand the situation.
5. Having followed Steps 2-4 for each of the opinions that you listed in Step 1 above, you have given yourself some freedom from the fixed opinions. How has your understanding expanded?
6. If the behaviour that you were judging was reflecting something that you don't like in your own past, in your character, or in your behaviour, what would it be reflecting?
7. What could you change in yourself so as not to be an example of or a part of what you are judging?
8. Steps 1-5 can be applied to expand understanding and compassion for any situation from a family argument to political conflict.

36. Exercises for Chapter 21: Vision

Exercise 21. The Castle In Your Mind: a Vision that makes a difference

You can use this exercise to expand your vision of the difference you can make, by creating a vision for a project or for your life. Our lives are limited by what we believe to be possible. Our well-trained minds restrict us from thinking 'outside the box'. This helps us to stay focused, but it may not help us to find joy and satisfaction.

Do this exercise with a pad of paper and pen ✐ to capture what you learn, alone, in a group, or with someone to coach or facilitate you. It is useful to write notes on paper as this focuses attention.

Use **A Simple Breath Meditation**, on page 120 to enter a ॐ meditative state, when the exercise asks you to imagine or explore. If you are coaching, your role is to remain in a loving ♥ state yourself and to support people in achieving a meditative and preferably sacred state from which to focus on the questions, rather than to help them to answer the questions.

Find a quiet time and space. Whenever you read 'imagine' in the exercise below, try to think, feel, see and hear, to involve all of your senses. When you imagine, you may not see a picture, but you may be able to imagine a sensation, sounds or thoughts of the future you are imagining.

STEP 1. ॐ Review your purpose in a meditative state ॐ

Take a few minutes with eyes closed, sitting upright in a simple meditation to become relaxed and to enhance your intuition and creativity.

Feel your purpose. Know that you are your purpose. Let go of your attachment to commitments and obligations and imagine that the only purpose of your life is to live your purpose. Let go of any expectations for the outcome of this exercise, for example by saying: "I surrender the outcome of this exercise to the good of all concerned. I surrender the outcome to love."

STEP 2. ✐Explore the difference you could make✐

If you had no fear or limitation:

What difference would you like to make in the world through this project or your life?

How would your life be as a part of making this difference, in terms of your happiness, success and fulfilment?

Write brief notes as a reminder for later steps.

STEP 3. ✿Imagine, feel, hear, think it already done!✿

Imagine having made the difference. It is already done. Think of the people who have benefited and the partners that helped you to make it happen. Smile. ☺ Feel the pride and satisfaction. Hear people thanking you for the difference you have made. See the scene of the difference you have made. Think of what it will do for the world and in your life. Make sure that the vision you are creating is a win for you *and* the world.

Who are the **partners** who helped you to make the difference? Imagine thanking them for their partnership and sharing the joy, pride and satisfaction.

Imagine looking back on your life and seeing how everything you experienced, even the hard times, helped you to learn and grow to make the difference that you made. You may like to list the major challenges of your life down the left-hand side of a piece of paper and on the right-hand side, write a sentence to explain how the challenge helped you to find or fulfil your purpose or vision.

STEP 4. ✐Crystallise your vision by writing it down✐

Describe on paper the difference that you have made as if it has already happened.

Use mind-maps, poetry, pictures, diagrams, photographs, whatever helps you – be creative and have fun!

How does the world work now?

What does the world look like, sound like, feel like now?

Who benefits and in what ways?

How does your life benefit in happiness, success and fulfilment?

STEP 5. ✌It was easy – it was already happening!✌

Meditate on your vision so it becomes clear in your mind. When the difference you have made and the happiness, success and fulfilment are present and real for you, now imagine that it feels very easy. It was going to happen anyway. It was already unfolding. You are not imagining, you are seeing the future, the future that is already happening. ☺ Smile or even laugh as you realise: "All that worry and concern and it was going to happen anyway!"

STEP 6. ✒Complete and expand your vision✒

If the future you have imagined is easy, then what can you achieve? Repeat from STEP 2 at least once and more if you feel the exercise will develop or expand your vision further. Each time you repeat, stretch your imagination to make more of a difference or to refine the vision of your contribution and your personal benefits in happiness, success and fulfilment.

STEP 7. ✒Create the Castle In Your Mind✒

Complete and perfect the description of your vision from STEP 4 as a beautiful document or picture that you can put on your wall or carry in your wallet. Think of it as the brochure, specification, plan or blueprint of a beautiful Castle In Your Mind that you can choose to build through your project or your life. You might like to add a caption to say something like: "This is my vision which I am magnetising and building through my life." In a meditative state, sign and date your vision with a quality of sacredness and commitment, as you might sign a marriage certificate. When you do this the power of your vision will be magnified many times. (See scientific papers on http://www. MindOfMany.com : "Intention when in a meditative state can shape reality".)

STEP 8. ⚘Meditate on the Castle In Your Mind⚘

Morning and evening go into a meditative state, for example using the Simple Breath Meditation. Imagine the Castle In Your Mind so that it becomes more and more real in your mind. The more real it becomes, the more you will attract synchronicity and magnetise your vision into reality. Practise visualising the Castle In Your Mind for 40 days morning and evening.

Practices are habits of behaviour. They become habits through the discipline of regular practice. Below, you will find two daily practices to support you in living your purpose and making your vision real.

Exercise 22. Creating Vision Cards

In this exercise, you create Vision Cards with affirmations that reflect the Castle In Your Mind. When you review these affirmations, they draw you into the future. When you review them daily, you become a magnet for your vision and your vision becomes your reality. If you do not use affirmations today, then try using vision cards for 40 days before you decide whether they work or not and choose whether to continue. Although this exercise focuses on physical cards, you could equally use the outputs of this exercise to create a screensaver for your computer or a looping recording to listen to on a tape player, CD player, computer or MP3 player. The more media you use, the better.

You will need a pad of paper and pen ✐ as usual *and* to complete the exercise, a thick, dark coloured pen ✐ and about 30 pieces of pale-coloured, good quality card. ▤ These cards will be used to write affirmations, so they should be big enough to allow you to write and easily read a sentence of up to about 12 words. The size of a business card or twice that size is a good size for Vision Cards. If you do not have cards to hand, you can fold and cut 4 sheets of A4 or US Letter writing paper into 8 pieces each to give 32 'cards'.

You can do this exercise either alone or with a partner to coach you. If you are coaching, your role is to remain in a loving ♥state yourself and to support people in achieving a meditative and preferably sacred state from which to focus on the exercise, rather than to help them to answer the questions.

Find a quiet time and space. Clear an area so that you can meditate vision and write as needed. A view of nature or beauty is helpful. If you are indoors, you can light a candle. Do what you need to do to give a sacred quality to your environment and actions.

STEP 1.   ✒Write down between 3 and 7 Life Areas✒

Choose Life Areas that are important to you and be sure that you include Health, Well-being or something similar. Other Life Areas might be "Family", "Work", "Making a Difference", "Money", "Relationship", "Friends", "Spiritual" etc. Choose areas that suit you and balance between your needs, your family needs, your contribution to others and between happiness and material success.

STEP 2.   ༀReview purpose and visionༀ

Take a few minutes with eyes closed, sitting upright in a simple meditation to become relaxed and to enhance your intuition and creativity.

Feel your purpose. Know that you are your purpose. Let go of your attachment to commitments and obligations and imagine that the only purpose of your life is to live your purpose. Let go of any expectations for the outcome of this exercise, for example by saying: "I surrender the outcome of this exercise to the good of all concerned. I surrender the outcome to love." Know that your vision is already happening. Imagine your vision, the Castle In Your Mind.

STEP 3. ✏ Create affirmation statements ✏

When the Castle In Your Mind is real, how is each Life Area affected?

For each Life Area, write from one to three affirmations to describe how that area is, now that your vision has been achieved. Ensure that your affirmations are in the present tense. It has already happened! Capture the clarity of the Castle In Your Mind. Capture the ease with which it was achieved. Write an affirmation that captures how it feels to be there already.

For example, in the area of 'Relationship', you might have envisioned meeting a life partner who is a companion and soul mate. You might use the affirmation: "I feel so blessed that I am with my soul mate now." The affirmation assumes that it has already happened. It brings the future into the present helping us to magnetise our vision into reality. Try different sentences until you find words that are simple and positive. You'll know that you have it right when you read a sentence and you feel inspired and motivated. Affirmation is a powerful tool and should be treated with respect. Never create an affirmation with the intention that another person, living thing, or nature will be harmed or denied the right of choice.

Here are further examples...

In the Life Area "Spiritual": Now that I meditate every day, I am naturally joyful, intuitive and calm.

Or "Now that I am living my purpose, I am blessed with miracles every day."

In the area of Money you might choose: "I am a catalyst for my vision and money flows easily into my life."

In the area of Health you might choose: "I am fit, strong and healthy, with an abundance of energy."

There is no right number of affirmations. Anything from one to three or four in each Life Area works well. If in doubt, start with less and add more affirmations when you feel you need to.

STEP 4. Review and adjust

Review the affirmations and adjust them until you feel you have a balance that reflects your vision. Make sure that no one would be harmed if your affirmations became reality.

STEP 5. Make your Vision Cards in a sacred manner

Now write your purpose on one card and each of the affirmations on separate Vision Cards in the thick dark coloured pen. Speak as you write. Write with intention. Imagine that what you are writing is already true and feel how it feels to be the person for whom it is true. Imagine that you are writing with a sacred pen on sacred paper and that what you write becomes real through the act of writing. Your Purpose answers the question WHY? These Vision Cards answer the question WHAT? In a subsequent exercise, you answer the question HOW?

STEP 6. Review your Vision Cards daily, read and experience

Review each of your Vision Cards at least once a day and preferably at least twice a day for 40 days. Read each card out loud (or quietly if in company), imagining that the affirmation is already true. Experience the affirmation with all your senses.

Vision Cards make your Vision tangible and physical.

Exercise 23. Creating Your Vision Plan

Use this exercise to create a path, road map, flow diagram or flow chart to take you step by step to your vision. This exercise uses a simple, powerful approach that applies equally to grounding a personal vision, planning a family project, developing a breakthrough business plan or developing a plan for a community.

Do this exercise with a pad of paper, flipchart or board and pen ✐ to capture what you learn. Use it alone, in a group, or with someone to coach or facilitate you. For this exercise, use a piece of paper turned on its side. (You may also want to have some transparent tape to hand if your paper turns out not to be wide enough!)

When this exercise asks you to imagine or explore, use the Simple Breath Meditation ࿘ for a few minutes to enter a meditative state. If you are coaching, your role is to remain in a loving ♥ state yourself and to support people in achieving a meditative and preferably sacred state from which to focus on the questions, rather than to help them to answer the questions.

Find a quiet time and space. Clear an area so that you can meditate, envision and write as needed. A view of nature or beauty is helpful. If you are indoors, you can light a candle. Do what you need to do to give a sacred quality to your environment and actions.

STEP 1. ࿘ Review your purpose and Vision Cards ࿘

Take a few minutes with eyes closed, sitting upright in a simple meditation to become relaxed and to enhance your intuition and creativity.

Review your purpose and vision using your Vision Cards. Know that you are your purpose. Imagine the 'Castle in Your Mind'. See your vision, hear it, feel it, think about it, as if you are living in the future where it is real already. Let go of any expectations for the outcome of this exercise, for example by saying: "I surrender the outcome of this exercise to the good of all concerned. I surrender the outcome to love."

STEP 2. ✒Draw an object for the Castle In Your Mind✒

On the right-most edge of the paper, draw an object, image or small box, representing the Castle In Your Mind. Label it with a few words above or below to describe your vision – capture the feeling and the idea, saying the words out loud. (Each time you draw a box to represent your vision in the rest of this exercise, use sounds, words, feelings and pictures as you did here.) Here is a simple example.

Example: Vision: My soul mate and I live in the home of our dreams.

STEP 3. What happened just before that

Imagine standing in the time when your vision is real and ask yourself two questions:
EVENT: What event happened to complete your vision?
Example: EVENT: We moved in.
STATE: What was the state or situation just before the vision was completed?
Example: STATE: Waiting to move in.

Add a box or picture to the left of the box representing your vision and an arrow connecting from the new box to the box describing your vision. Label the line with a few words describing the event. Then label the second box to describe how the world looked just before this event happened.

STEP 4. Repeat to track back from vision to present

Repeat steps 2-3 until you have traced the steps from fulfilment of your vision, back to current day reality. Review the steps taken as if you were remembering how your vision came about.

STEP 5. Review from the present to the vision

Now review the steps that you have taken, starting with current day reality and imagine them happening forwards in time. Refine the steps if you need to until they make sense as a plan for creating your vision. Remember that it is not up to us to build our vision single-handed, but it is up to us to make it real in our minds, so that we are ready to recognise the people and circumstances magnetised towards us to make it real. You may not yet have met the people you need to meet to fulfil your vision. That's OK. You can even label some of the steps as 'miracles' if they require a leap of faith. (Check the dictionary definition of a miracle if you are uncomfortable with this word, then choose a word that suits you.) Think of this plan as the way that the Castle In Your Mind will be built through your life. How does it serve your purpose? How does it happen? How does it work, look, feel, sound?

STEP 6. Your Vision Plan

What would need to happen by when for your Vision Plan to become real? Set dates for beginning and end points. Set milestones and specific goals and targets that can be measured and reviewed on a weekly, monthly or quarterly basis. Although the process is not described in this book, you can develop a "Scorecard" to visualise progress of your Vision Plan.

STEP 7. Summarise into Vision Plan and Vision Cards

Summarise the diagram onto a piece of paper to show the path by which the Castle In Your Mind will be built and into one or more Vision Cards. (See: Creating Vision Cards on page 155)

Keep the piece of paper showing your Vision Plan, where you work, in your diary, where you sleep or in a notebook that you refer to regularly. Add the Vision Cards to those describing the Castle In Your Mind.

STEP 8. Review your Vision Plan and Vision Cards daily

Morning and evening when you review your Vision Cards, or when you meditate, visualise your Vision Plan becoming real, being reality. If you have a scorecard visualise the colours changing indicating that everything is becoming complete. (See: Visualisation Practice on page 162.) Imagine that you have already fulfilled your vision and are remembering how it happened and how it felt. Imagine the steps of your plan unfolding from the future into the present. Then imagine the steps happening from the present into the future. Involve all of your senses.

Exercise 24. Visualisation Practice

Preferably find a regular time for this practice, for example morning before getting up and each evening before sleep. This only need take a few minutes. Keep a pen and pad of paper beside you to capture any insights that you may have during the practice.

STEP 1. Find a quiet time and space, relax and breathe

Review the Vision Cards for your Purpose, your Vision and your Vision Plan.

Relax and breathe for one minute, surrendering any concerns or worries that you may have. Be aware of the rhythm of your breath in your body and nothing else. Surrender. Feel your belly rise and fall as you breathe. If ever you are distracted, surrender and bring your attention back to your breath. Relax. (With practice, you will find this relaxation and surrender easier and easier.)

STEP 2. Focus attention on your 'third eye'

When you are relaxed, bring your attention to a point on your forehead just above the meeting point of your eyebrows. In eastern traditions, this is called the third eye, seat of your vision. Imagine that you are seeing from your third eye. Notice if you see any visions or pictures.

Now imagine that as you breathe, you are breathing in and out of your third eye.

STEP 3. Visualise the Castle In Your Mind

With your attention and breath focused on your third eye, imagine your Vision; see 'The Castle in Your Mind' through your third eye until it feels real to all of your senses.

STEP 4. Follow your Vision Plan from future to present

Follow the steps of your Vision Plan back from your Vision, to the present day. Imagine each step on the way until it feels real to all of your senses. Imagine nodding your head very gently and smiling as you 'remember' the unfolding of your Vision Plan. Now follow the steps of

your Vision Plan from the present day to fulfilment of your Vision. Imagine each step on the way until it feels real to all of your senses.
1. Begin to return from the depth and concentration of your meditation and just breathe for three minutes or as long as you need to return to normal consciousness.
2. Begin to smile very gently as you perceive the beauty of your Vision and 'remember' the unfolding of your Vision Plan as if it has already happened. Now nod your head very gently and know that your Vision is already real and is already unfolding.

STEP 5.   Review your Vision Cards

Read each of your Vision cards in turn, holding the smile on your face and maintaining a relaxed and meditative state.

STEP 6.   Return from meditation

Sit quietly for two minutes, and then begin to wiggle your toes and rub your fingers, then stretch and move your muscles and gently open your eyes when you feel you are ready. Sit quietly again until you are ready to move.

Part I: Purpose and Vision

I. Notes on My Journey

Perhaps this book shaped me before I wrote it, or perhaps I shaped it based on my experience. Here is how the book found its way through me.

My parents saw the end of the Second World War in their early twenties. They carried with them a hope and expectation of a better, fairer world. I was born into that expectation in Cardiff in Wales, a part of the United Kingdom in 1961. I grew up in a loving home, which was not religious.

When I am 7, my father dies and I discover that my mother is not boundless in her strength. I make it mean that I have to grow up there and then and be the solution to problems.

At 10, I am afraid that one day I'll have to do a job that is boring.

At 12 I leave the boy scouts because I can't promise service to a God I don't know.

At 13, because I cannot, with honesty, make the promises involved in Christian confirmation, I leave the church choir although I love the way that the music makes me feel.

At 14, along with the other things teenagers fall in love with, I begin to fall in love with science.

I can never find the motivation to memorise facts just because I am meant to know them.

I argue with a girl I love, that everything in the universe is determined. And in a world of science, there is no room for God. You could say that science has become the religion of my childhood.

In studying sciences, I find I can see patterns behind ideas that make the ideas seem easy.

At 18 I go to Oxford University. It is my highest aspiration at the time. I go to Oxford to study medicine.

165

(Both my parents were medical researchers and teachers. My father was also a physician.)

Four weeks later, I quit. Two things had happened. First, they ask me to remember every muscle in the body and I can find no motivation to do it. Second, I ask a question in a lecture and am told that I do not need to understand the answer to be a doctor. This is like saying you don't need to know about God to be a priest so I quit. My mother, my best friend by this time, is very disappointed. "I thought you'd be a great doctor like your father…"

At 19, if I'm not going to be a doctor, I'd like to find out about computers, but they don't really have a course on that at Oxford yet. I change to study engineering as the nearest thing I can find!

The next summer my mother dies. I discover depths of experience that I have never known. I realise how much I love her. I am consoled by irrational thoughts.

I see the image in my mind of a white dove, released into flight by caring hands. To me the image is clear: "Your mother was there until you came of age, while you still needed her and now that you can take care of yourself, she has left. It's better that way." Where did the picture come from? I don't know, but it makes me feel better. I am still grieving, but more than anything else I feel love. There is another image too. It is of a tulip flower. It helps me with the sad thought that my mother has died before her life has blossomed, just before she planned a working trip to Africa to help to build a new medical school. The message in the tulip image is: "You are the blossom. Go on and live your life. Make the flower. Be the flower."

Over the next few years I meet some completely inexplicable phenomena. I have to revisit my world-view. How come intuition works? In my early 20s, I study briefly with David Bohm, the physicist, who is teaching at a spiritual community in England. His deep, intuitive understanding of physical and spiritual reality helps my mind and my intuition to meet.

I've always been joyful, but now I become more intensely aware of my love of nature, of life. I find myself consciously aware of a connection with everything. I feel myself as a conduit of love and Universal power.

I start in business and find challenges that drive me to ask a higher power for help. I receive extraordinary guidance and support. The science of my youth cannot explain what I now experience. My company seems to have great promise. After it fails in 1990, I realise that I didn't believe that the Universe would let this happen to me. (Now that thought makes me laugh! The words that come to my mind, delivered warmly and with compassion are "The Universe doesn't care about your feelings, it cares about your purpose!") These are difficult times for me and for the people who depend on me. So, what is the blessing? I learn some humility. Before that, I realise that I thought that if a person was not materially successful then they were not somehow spiritually valuable. I had lived in my own reality in two ways.

1. I thought that the Universe or God cared about my ego's desire to be successful.
2. I had my own reality in which I believed it would all turn out.

Now I can know deeply that the degree of material success that a person has achieved is no indication of their spiritual worth.

How I'd describe it now is that the Universe denied me what I most wanted (success) to give me what I most needed to grow spiritually (humility and grounding or a dose of material reality). It cost me my apartment in London and led me into some fairly meagre financial times. It had a cost to people close to me too. It took 5 years for me to complete paying off the resulting debts. Looking back now, that just seems like another ripple in the sea of Universal cause and effect, or what is called in the East karma, which I perceive as pervading life. Karma is so beautifully simple.

In 1994, a relationship of 5 years ends. I've behaved badly. Again, I've lived in my own reality. When I come to see what I have done in the real world, rather than in my world, for the first time in my life I experience real guilt. It is horrible, disgusting, and unquenchable. I cannot take back what I have done. It will not go away.

As a part of a long process I take a week off work and spend a large part of it crying. Instead of easing, the feelings get stronger, the more I look into the eye of what has happened. I try letting the other person go. That works to a degree, but it doesn't weaken my sense of guilt. Somehow, an intuitive understanding of karma teaches me what to do. I've read that anger is "a way of making someone else feel guilty." I choose to give up the right to make other people feel guilty. I choose to give up the right to anger. It is a kind of karmic pact. It works. It also completely changes my life. Before this, I'd become angry and resentful. I was judgemental. I would spend a lot of my time in a kind of righteous bad temper – being too busy.

Actually, I think I was just ashamed of where my life had got to. Anyway, giving up the right to be angry was amazing. I found love returning to my life, all of it, most of the time. I enjoyed letting people know that I would fully and finally forgive them. (I now realise that to make my mark in the world, I must also maintain boundaries as well as forgiving.) Overall, this most painful experience gave me the gift of forgiveness and gave me back the

Part I: Purpose and Vision

experience of love. It lost me reciprocation of a love whose memory I will treasure for the rest of my life.

This is a high price to pay for awareness. Again, karma is ruthless with my delusions. As time goes by, I realise I'm angry with the Universe and trying to get my own back by continuing to achieve very little. This seems pretty funny now. My conclusion is that the Universe does not respond to temper tantrums, but it takes some time to learn this lesson!

This book is an answer to a prayer. It's mid 1999. Somehow, I find myself looking back on 38 years of aspiration, life and work and feeling that a part of me, my passion, my commitment, my love, has not made its mark through my life. I've been spending time now for over six months, contemplating my life, my purpose, looking for a meaning beyond my everyday life and work. The Purpose Exercise I offer to other people works fine for me too, but I can't see a connection between the life I have and the purpose I'm given by the exercise. I want to change the world, but struggle to build my small business.

Events, visions, messages and disappointments, but still no real breakthrough... I say a prayer and get a dramatically clear message in response. "Meditate, contemplate, listen to your inner voice. Get on with it!" I meditate intentionally, morning and night. I go to a Step Aerobics class in late 2000 only to find with disappointment that it is a yoga class. Even in the first class I can feel the power of the exercises on my body's energy system. Kundalini Yoga becomes a regular part of my exercise practice, particularly the simple exercise referenced on www.MindOfMany.com.

It is February 2000. I've only just completed the book I've been writing on business performance management, called "Managing in the New Economy, Renewing Organisations for the New Millennium" – the same book as has been more recently published in Japanese under the name "Balanced Scorecard Best Practice". The contemplation starts to work. I start to see patterns. I wonder if I'm making it up, or if there really is a pattern to my life. I've seen patterns before.

I'm flying to Brussels. I'm reading what turns out to be an uninspiring business book that I have bought at the airport. The title sounded great, but the book is not catching my interest. My mind wanders as I read the book. It is hard to describe what happens. Words start to come into my mind. I am imagining a website: "Do we dare to enter on a journey of transformation that might just change the world." I write the words down in the margin of the book; in the only pen I can find which is green.

What follows is like pulling a piece of spaghetti. As I write each sentence, the next sentence forms in my mind. Things seem to fit together. By the time we land, the inside front and back covers of the book are filled in green writing and the margins of several pages are filled too.

Over the next few months, whenever my mind is quiet, or in the middle of the night, I continue to get insights that unravel as I write them down. Since then, I've spent time organising the contents. This book (Part 1) is about a third of the total. I love that it makes sense both to my intuition and to my scientific mind. This book has become a guide and companion to me.

Karma forces me to care about material things, because it is too unbearable to live a life where I make no difference. Karma forces me to develop and maintain my personal boundaries as well as just forgiving everything without a thought for next time. Without boundaries, I am impotent and it is too unbearable to be impotent in a world where I see the need for change. I torture myself with visions that are unfulfilled and in this way, karma forces me to become better at getting things done, as well as just seeing what needs to be done. Karma constantly, reliably and ruthlessly corrects me.

I do experience life as filled with miracles, for which I am very grateful. I have shared an example in "Seven Days in Japan", which is the diary of a week I spent in Japan in June 2001.

For me, the value in this book is that it illuminates the pattern of the extraordinary time at which we live. My experience is that many, many of us are coming to a new level of awareness now. Somehow, the answers that worked in the past don't seem sufficient any more. I believe that this is the spiritual gravity of the Emerging Global Transformation calling us to be courageous, to be extraordinary.

This book is a gift for anyone feeling the call of the soul. In spring 2005, I completed all of the Exercises from start to finish and found it a profoundly transforming process. I offer the book and exercises to you in humility.

II. Seven Days in Japan
Kaizen in the workplace, fireflies in Kyoto, Saint Francis of Assisi in a Buddhist temple and the secrets of Green Tea.

Travelling to Japan

I leave on Tuesday lunchtime and will arrive in Japan tomorrow, Wednesday. I've never flown this route before and I have never been to Japan. I can feel that this will be different. I'm excited and slightly apprehensive. I'm used to Europe and the US, but Japan is unknown to me.

We fly over the Bay of Finland, Archangelsk, the Ural Mountains and the Siberian Lowlands. Known and unknown names sound mystery and intrigue as we fly over the once forbidden territory of the former USSR. We are flying around the North of China a whole continent so different from what I know.

One of the movies catches my interest and I watch it before sleeping. Thirteen Days tells the story of the Cuba Missile Crisis, when the world held its breath as two superpowers balanced on the line between Détente and War. The story shows how fear pressed JFK, Bobby Kennedy and their clear-thinking advisor Kenny towards war and how they dared to make ethical decisions. By daring to look into the mind of the 'enemy' they were able to resist war.

To me, it showed that clear, more holistic thinking and resisting the temptation of fear, perhaps literally saved the world for the generation that we now enjoy. Kevin Costner's character Kenny showed non-judgement and compassion for the adversary of which a Buddhist would be proud. As a consequence, he had access to the understanding to make good decisions. This is a reflection of the spiral of Knowledge and Compassion.

Part 1: Purpose and Vision

In the last two years, I have been introduced to a military model for decision making, used both in the UK and the USA: the OODA Loop describes the cycle of Observe-Orient-Decide-Act by which decisions are made. The quality of decisions depends on the quality of the OODA Loop. Decision Superiority is the next military focus after Information Superiority. The speed of decisions depends on the speed of the OODA Loop. High quality, speedy decisions provide a key to military power now and in the future. The film showed that the players had the choice to short-circuit the Observe and Orient steps knee-jerking into Actions that would likely escalate to war. By Observing and Orienting from a larger perspective – understanding the pressures influencing the 'enemy' and by appreciating the potential global consequences of Mutually Assured Destruction, potential war was averted.

The story touched me. By changing the OODA Loop by which we conduct our decision making, we can keep the world safe. For me, the film confirmed that we live in a world where military success cannot only be purchased through more hardware and software, but through developing the thinking that operates in people's minds during decision making. (In the community in which I work professionally to improve and support improved strategic and operational decision making we have coined the term Cultureware, to describe this.)

I sleep on these thoughts and more for a few hours, wondering what the Ural Mountains and Archangelsk would look like if it were not now dark outside.

In Tokyo Masatoshi Hiroura meets me. Although we do not know much about one another, we are friends as well as colleagues. When I first met Masa, as a part of our conversation he completed a Values Assessment, which shows the values from which a person lives and what values they aspire to in their organisation. (See the website for Richard Barrett below for background to this assessment.) It became obvious that we shared the motivation to build a better world as well as build healthy businesses. Masatoshi runs FB Triangle and has arranged translation into Japanese of my company's products and my book on performance management. At the broadest level, our products help organisations to get better at getting better.

They include software and Cultureware. Cultureware describes the culture, practices and learning materials to embed 'getting better at getting better' into an organisation. FB Triangle specialises in Quality Management, selling products and services to support quality improvement. The Japanese for improvement is 'kaizen'. The kanji for kaizen is made up of two kanji characters: Kai (change) and (Zen) good feeling. On the bus ride into Tokyo we share thoughts about the OODA Loop. We talk about how it relates to the 5-Element-Cycle which is a foundation of Chinese Medicine. We talk about how it relates to the PDCA (Plan-Do-Check-Act) cycle of Quality Management. We talk about how changing the OODA Loop can change the world.

We talk about President Bush choosing not to proceed with the Kyoto Agreement on the environment. We talk of Yin and Yang: how when something becomes very positive, it then transitions to the opposite, for example vigorous exercise is followed by rest. Perhaps the pendulum needs to swing a little further against the environment, before there will be sufficient pressure to force a flip-over to positive change.

At FB Triangle's offices, I see the new Japanese brochures for our products and get a demo of our product in Japanese. David, my partner of 16 years and friend for more than half my life, will be proud to see all this. So will all our colleagues who have worked to make it happen.

FB Triangle has arranged two seminars to introduce Balanced Scorecard and our products for people from business, government and consultants. Tomorrow is Tokyo. The next day is Fukuoka.

Masa shows me my presentation translated into Japanese and printed out. We sit down to work through what will be presented by Masa and the other speaker. The other speaker, Matsubara San is a leading Japanese expert and author on performance management and the Balanced Scorecard. He is a key person in the Japanese Balanced Scorecard Forum.

We look at the pictures together and Masa translates the context. I like the holistic way in which Matsubara San sees the subject. He takes into account both planning and implementing. He uses analogies from nature – saying that the organisation is like a tree bearing fruits. It is not enough to just gather the fruits (count the money). An organisation must take care of its foliage for gathering sunlight (customer service), its trunk and branches (processes) and also its roots (the learning and growth of its people).

This subject, business performance management and transformation, seems to draw like-minded people who want to make organisations work better. I'm looking forward to meeting Matsubara San.

Challenging times for Japan

Japan is in a challenging time. After years of extraordinary, seemingly unending growth, the economy is in recession and has been for 10 years. The interlocking ownership of companies that helped to propel the growth was also a seed for problems. The Japanese government had to bail out the banking system leaving a debt of about

£40,000 ($60,000) per Japanese citizen that will need to be paid off through taxes in the future. A new Prime Minister is in place with overwhelming 80% popular approval. While he is by old demarcations a conservative, he seems to be thinking in liberal ways.

It all reminds me of the Tony Blair government in the UK. The need to modernise, a 'New Labour' government doing 'Conservative' things to try and build the financial stability on which social progress can be made. It also reminds me of our experience and learning from working on Best Value in UK government. The Best Value legislation provides a positive vision for how government can do a good job at building a better society and world. The Best Value legislation makes it an obligation to demonstrate continuous improvement in 'economic, social and environmental outcomes'. It is a great idea, but it is not proving easy. All the vision, intention and money may not make a difference. In the UK I've worked with many people on this and spoken with hundreds of people. Turning vision and money into results is not easy.

To me this seems like the challenge of our next government in the UK. As one civil servant put it early last year: "How do we change the culture of the civil service? How do we galvanise change?" In the UK, we are building a community to work together on these questions.

It would be nice to be able to take all of the learnings from working on this in the UK and to provide these to Japanese government employees working on the same issues. With this in mind, there are numerous government people coming to the two seminars, so it is important that we understand the background.

The next day at the seminar, I am able to tie my presentation back to Matsubara San's introduction. We talk about alignment, kaizen and implementation (making

Part I: Purpose and Vision

things happen). We honour how the Japanese were able to apply the power of quality management to create one of the world's greatest ever economic success stories. We plant seeds in people's minds that performance management and Balanced Scorecard may be the key to taking organisations on past their current challenges. The response is good.

At dinner that night we east sushi, abalone and sea urchin. We agree that it would be interesting to involve, for example, a Zen Buddhist in helping to shape the Japanese Balanced Scorecard Forum's development of best practice in performance management. It turns out that Matsubara San went to a Zen Buddhist school. A door opens. We don't look inside too deeply, but I am sure we will.

Matsubara San, Masa and I have aligned thoughts – to provide a curriculum and tools to help people and organisations to apply all of these ideas. It seems important. It seems timely. Matsubara San acknowledges my knowledge of Japanese culture. We talk about how Buddhism might have something to teach our search for best practice in performance management and development of organisations.

The next day, we leave for Fukuoka at 5am. We fly over the folded mountains of Japanese islands. On the flight I read in a newspaper about how Japan has recommitted itself to the Kyoto Agreement and how the new government intends (to use a British term) to modernise local government.

Our seminar is at 1pm. Today, the other presenter is Itchkara San, an expert in Quality Management. We meet and review his presentation together. Masa translates. Itchkara San shows the need for Japanese businesses to move on from the Kyoritsu (clubs of connected businesses) model to create alliances along value chains.

It talks about the requirements of different quality standards, especially in relation to the environment. It seems that Japan is adopting high standards in relation to environmental impact. We talk about how Japanese businesses will reap the rewards when other countries inevitably follow the legislative path to environmental stewardship. Japanese organisations will be ready with systems and products for compliance.

I am reminded of President Bush's recent decision not to commit to the Kyoto Agreement on the grounds that it would harm US economic interests. Perhaps the environmentalists will inherit the earth after all. I can imagine a world where the Japanese and others will be selling and licensing their environmental solutions to other nations.

I meet my translator. After she has reviewed my printed presentation, we get talking. I start to become aware of the depth and archaeology represented by the Japanese kanji characters. Depth, in that words are often made up of other words. For example, the kanji for business is made up of the kanji for planning and doing. The kanji for government is made up of the kanji for governing and planning. Archaeology, in that kanji characters show derivations of meaning. For example, the kanji character for a person represents two people, one leaning on the other, showing that none of us can exist on our own. What subliminal effect does all of this richness have on people as they read and communicate using these characters? The seminar starts. Today in the audience we have business and government people, including a city politician. I give a different presentation today, although the slides are the same.

Someone from the Japanese Research Institute asks a question about implementation, culture, motivation and rewards. I've heard the same question in slightly different form three weeks running. Last week at the European Balanced Scorecard Summit in Nice, it seemed to be the key area for success of Balanced Scorecard. The week before at the CorpTools user conference in North Carolina, we talked about intrinsic and extrinsic motivation. I am in awe that the same questions, the same conversations and the same challenges are top-of-mind across three continents in governments, businesses and the military.

That night at dinner with Itchkara San and Masa, we talk about the 'movement' of Balanced Scorecard, of Quality and of transformation of organisations. We talk about the magnetic quality of a human being aligned with their purpose. We talk about the seminar theme of alignment of organisations – lining up the resources of everyone in an organisation so that the organisation as a whole can create and do more. We talk about how organisations working across a supply chain and in alliances must find ways to align and how organisations that are not aligned internally will find it hard to make strategic alliances externally. We talk about fractals – patterns in nature that repeat at multiple levels - the patterns in clouds that seem the same when magnified. Fractals are used in computer generation of natural scenes. A very simple fractal 'attractor' or formula can generate a complex mountain range.

We talk about how an organisation, a supply chain, or a nation that is internally aligned is then naturally pulled into alignment with the movements or trends around it. It all seems to fit together – the movement towards environmental organisations and the alignment of organisations to play their part in that movement. We talk about people being magnetic and shining as examples of what they stand for. The conversation is liberating and inspiring. It seems as though all that has happened in the day fits together.

In my briefcase, I find a card depicting Saint Francis of Assisi. I have always been inspired by his love of, and communing with, nature and by his personification of purity and peace. I offer it to Masa as a gift, explaining briefly who Saint Francis was.

Tomorrow is Saturday. We will be 'on holiday', I think. My first thought is "great, I can finally get some sleep", but that doesn't feel like the right thing, so we agree to be up early again.

Hiroshima: city of peace

The next morning we set off early for Hiroshima. I have no idea what we will see.

I have no explanation for how Hiroshima touches me, but it does. As I step off the train at Hiroshima station, emotion begins to well up inside me. The words 'how could we do this?' came into my mind. By the time we reach the escalator tears are trickling down my cheeks. I don't think that anyone notices. We leave our luggage in the station lockers.

The Hiroshima peace museum tells the story of what happened factually, holistically, with compassion and without blame.

The museum traces the history of the city of Hiroshima as a manufacturing and supply station for military campaigns. The display boards pick out events that tell a story of increasing intensity of focus on this military purpose. Filling in the moat which had circled the old city, to provide more space for military buildings, melting down of street lamps to forge weaponry, training and drilling children for military work and finally on the day of the bomb, a school is being demolished to create an effective firebreak. After centuries as a supply point for

Part I: Purpose and Vision

military operations into South East Asia, at this moment of ultimate military focus, the bomb was dropped shortly after an air raid warning had been lifted. Thousands of people died in a moment and the city was laid to waste. From aggressive focus to ultimate vulnerability in that moment.

The museum also describes the seemingly clinical criteria by which American generals chose their target. It invokes the unspeakable atrocity of the result through photographs, melted metal and ceramics, the shadow of a person captured by the nuclear flash on the stone steps of a bank. Finally, testimonials from survivors complete the picture. This really happened. Different people, in different places, none judged as intrinsically bad, created a scar on humanity and our planet.

A place that had, for so long, prepared for and supported war, became its ultimate victim. A nation that had built its total commitment to victory on the belief of invincibility was brought to humility through an event that lasted a few seconds. A device developed from deep investigation into the nature of reality and matter, a pinnacle of humanity's science and technology, had been used to implement a previously unimaginable inhumanity - mass, impersonal destruction of people, nature and place. All this invoked earlier discussions of Yin and Yang: the extreme of anything gives way to its opposite and karma: cause and effect. A city built on war and destruction becoming its ultimate victim.

Hiroshima is not a place of despair. It is a place of extraordinary compassion, hope and love. As the focus for one of humanity's great inhumanities, Hiroshima and its people have created and stand for a vision of a world without nuclear weapons and ultimately, a world of peace. Each time a nuclear test is carried out anywhere in the world, the mayor of Hiroshima writes to the president of that country with a request that it be the last. Each year on the anniversary of the bomb of August 6th 1945, Hiroshima holds a world memorial dedicated to world peace. 50,000 people attended in August 2000.

Like the person who inspires by having learned from bitter experience, Hiroshima deeply moves and inspires me as a city for it has learned and stands for the possibility of peace. In an act of great generosity and leadership, Hiroshima and Nagasaki offer to be the only cities to experience Nuclear weapons. They offer us the possibility of peace without having to learn through devastation.

As I write this, I am very aware of the Christian story of the Christ dying on the cross so that we might be forgiven. To use other terms, Hiroshima and Nagasaki were part of the cause and effect, or in eastern terms, karma of a city, a nation and our planet. Karma completes itself and delivers purification. In Christian terms, when we sin and then repent of our sins, we are purified. There is purity to the way in which the Hiroshima museum describes what happened which is a treasure for all of humanity.

The last part of the museum includes a globe showing where nuclear warheads are stacked. I notice, in the UK, the US, France and China. As I walk out of the display area, Masa is waiting.

We share very few words.

"I find it very sad" I say, my voice breaking.

He leads me over to sit down.

I give up the effort not to cry as I speak. I thank Masa for bringing me here and he confirms that he knew that it would be something that I would want to feel. Masa was last here at the age of 20, over 20 years ago. On his first visit, he saw the atrocity and the waste. On this visit, more of a pattern has revealed itself. We are united in our experience and sit together for a while.

Part I: Purpose and Vision

I would recommend anyone to go to Hiroshima and visit this monument. Hiroshima gives its experience and history as a gift to humanity that we can all use in building peace – peace in ourselves and peace in our world.

We walk from the museum into the city. Two joyful, young teenagers are making music on the bridge into the city. We spend a few moments with a monument the "Angel of Peace" and looking at the dome of a building preserved in its damaged state as a monument to past destruction. We eat in the town and take a taxi to the station.

Kyoto

On the Shinkansen or Bullet Train from Hiroshima to Kyoto, we talk. In preparing our seminars, Masa asked me to be careful about using the word culture. Masa explains. Culture means the old way, the tradition. Tradition and the old way have become entangled with the manipulation and abuse that was used to keep the Japanese at war. Now people are wary of the word culture. It is tarnished with the danger of remaking past mistakes.

Masa comes from a Buddhist family, but his wife and children are Catholic. He is at a crossing point of two cultures. In Japan, there is a history of the established religions being manipulated for political ends, whereas the people involved in Christianity appear more trustworthy.

For my part, I was raised in a Christian culture, but I am aware of historical abuse of the pure Christian message, for example in the Spanish Inquisition and more recently in revelations about the church covering up child abuse by priests. I have been exposed to a long list that has made me wary of the trustworthiness of my own culture's religious institutions. On the other hand, I do not have the same baggage with regard to Buddhism, for example.

We realise that there is potential for each of us to mistrust the religion of our childhood because we have seen it abused. It seems as though there is a pattern to all that we have experienced from considering the status of the Japanese economy, government and national self-confidence, to the importance of the environment and how things might change. Also in the key role of performance management and quality management in building a better world.

It dawns on us that we are heading for Kyoto, the place where the Kyoto Agreement was created. This seems to be more of the same pattern of coincidences.

In Kyoto, we visit a temple where 1,000 images of the Buddha stand together; each has tools in their hands to take away human suffering and to bring joy and happiness. It feels very different to the feeling in a church. The energy of the landscape is also different from places that I know. I remember having the same feeling when I was in Bali and also being in the United States, as if the way that the landscape lives and works is different.

I believe that every place has its secrets that we can come to know, if we know how to listen. I say a silent prayer to be able to see, feel and understand the wisdom of the ancient traditions of which these temples are a part. I read the information available in English, but it doesn't reveal anything of why things are the way they are, just what happened and when. I buy a mandala depicting a pattern of Buddhas.

Next we go to another temple, walking up high, then down the mountain past wells and through woodlands and gardens. We wash and drink from a well – symbolically to purify actions and words.

A 350-year-old restaurant

That evening, we eat at a tiny, beautiful restaurant. The façade is simple – dark-coloured wood with a low front door and a curtain. We enter and are greeted then we remove our shoes. The atmosphere inside is still and quiet. We are shown to a waiting room with paper walls and a sliding door. We sit and wait.

The restaurant has been in the same family for 350 years, with 10 generations of fathers and sons learning how to prepare exquisite food.

In a few minutes we are shown into a square room with four tatami mats arranged around a square central table at shin height with two cushions placed ready for us. First we are offered a cup of green tea with the ornate, formal practices of the tea ceremony. The tea is delicious, rich and frothy. Masa shows me how to hold and rotate the bowl through 45 degrees two times. How to hold it up in honour and then to drink it to the last, slurping as a polite and practical way to get the last froth from the bowl. He points out how our hostess asks before entering, then slides open the door with both hands while kneeling, then steps inside and kneels again to close it. She then stands up, walks the three steps to our table and kneels again to serve us. Every movement is prescribed.

We are given the menu written in kanji by the chef and barely legible to Masa because of its stylised artistic presentation. Of course, it is totally illegible to me. We are to enjoy 14 courses.

Each of the courses includes anything from one or two to nine different dishes. Nothing is in excess. Everything is simple, delicate and ornate. I ask Masa what the different dishes are and through the successive visits by our hostess, we learn more about the food and the restaurant. The current owner and chef is only 36 and the woman who is serving us is his wife. We feel that we are participating in an ancient tradition. The meal has a sacred quality.

When we finally leave, we thank our hostess, bowing and returning bows. As we leave sight of her, she is still kneeling in the entrance. If there was not such great dignity in her behaviour, it might be embarrassing, instead, it is beautiful, humbling and uplifting.

As we walk away, I am in a kind of dream state.

We talk about how we have now been shown the richness of Japanese tradition as if this tradition and ancient knowledge has something to offer to the transformation of organisations that we are witnessing and want to participate in. There seems to be a connection between the themes of environmental renewal, Kyoto as the home of the Kyoto agreement and our rich experience of Japanese tradition – as if they are all parts of an emergent whole.

Message of the fire flies

As we are walking, we pass three people on a bridge. They call and beckon us. I don't know what they are saying, but Masa says to come and look

How beautiful. They are excitedly showing us fireflies moving above and around the stream. They are excited because the fireflies had gone and now are back – a sign that the river water in Kyoto is becoming clean again. We watch as the fireflies are attracted towards one another by their light. I am reminded of the words of Nelson Mandela: "As we allow our light to shine we allow others to do the same." The more we think about it, the more power there is in the metaphor. We are the fireflies. These fireflies are able to see one another because they allow themselves to shine. We must allow ourselves to shine, for then we will discover the others with whom we can work to light up the world.

It has been an extraordinary and beautiful day, starting in Fukuoka, travelling to Hiroshima and ending here in the beautiful historic city of Kyoto. It feels as if we are on a magical, guided journey. We feel very blessed.

We return to the station and pick up our bags. Now to find our hotel... On the way there, we discover that we are staying close to the conference centre where the Kyoto Agreement was made. Later, we discover that we are staying in the conference hotel where the world leaders attending the conference stayed. Finally, we are both given room upgrades because we have arrived at 11.30 and all the standard rooms are taken. I'm in a palatial suite, probably where one of the government leaders would have stayed while at the conference.

The next day we will be visiting temples in Kyoto, so we agree to wake up early again.

In the morning we meet at 7. We leave our bags at Kyoto station and take a bus to our first temple of the day. During the 45-minute journey, I watch the Japanese children playing with their DoCoMo mobile phones. We wind up into the hills.

The Home of Green Tea

We enter Kozan-Ii temple, Taganoo, which is renowned for the beautiful scrolls showing frolicking animals and for being the temple that brought green tea to Japan. It is also the first Buddhist temple to form a link with a Catholic organisation. In 1986, it formed a link with a Franciscan order. The guidebook shows two pictures side by side: one of Saint Francis surrounded by animals and birds and the other of Buddhist monks, meditating in a tree. Just as Saint Francis of Assisi is known for his love of nature, these monks depict animals at play. Instead of formal Zen gardens with raked gravel and placed rocks, their gardens are wild. They believe in allowing nature to shape itself. It reminds me of my garden in Yorkshire. Finding ourselves in this temple reminds us of both the environmental theme and again the theme of crossing over between Buddhism and Christianity.

We walk around the temple, stopping to look out over the trees in front. I take a few moments at the altar and say a silent prayer to be connected to the wisdom of the place. A throng of children joins us. We look at the scrolls of frolicking animals. It is noisy. We move on and out. I stop and buy various reproductions of the animal art. I like its style and energy and feel it will go well at home in Yorkshire.

This is the Buddhist temple that brought green tea from China to Japan. Tea is cultivated here. Masa explains that the tea is very special. We stop and experience a tea ceremony. It starts with the now familiar sweet, but wrapped in paper depicting a rabbit at play. We follow the protocol of lifting the bowl, rotating it twice, holding it up in reverence and then drinking. The tea is wonderful, rich and frothy. We enjoy it quietly. I do the polite thing and loudly suck out the last of the froth from my bowl.

Now we leave the temple and walk out into the wider gardens, then up into the woodland above the temple. I find occasional pieces of litter and, following a habit that Gina and I have developed in the countryside at home, I collect it in a carrier bag. Masa thanks me. I explain that it is a habit from home; a kind of way of honouring nature and that nature often repays it with gifts. (Several hundred pounds worth of paving stones dumped outside our gate one time in Yorkshire for example.)

Eventually, we return down into the valley of the temples and gardens, walking down beautiful stone steps and along a causeway.

Meeting the Tea Spirit

Midges are flying directly into my eyes as we walk. No sooner than I have blinked one out, another flies in. It doesn't seem to bother Masa. The magical quality of the place has me question: "what does this mean?" The answer comes straight back to me. Look with your inner eye, your intuition, not with your eyes. I smile. Still with my eyes closed, I begin to try to sense intuitively. The whole place now feels alive. The stone steps down the causeway seem to dance with life – the same energy and vitality as the frolicking animals. My prayer has been answered – with a fly in the eye!

As we walk, we notice a beautiful rough stone about thigh height with a smoothed, flat surface cut into it and a pattern of artful kanji cut into this surface. I ask Masa to translate. It takes some time. The words simply say, reading from right to left: evening time, tea, and spirit. They suggest that at evening time the Tea Spirit is here. Yet when I look at the pattern, it seems more poetic. The kanji follow a pattern from right to left... Starting with an ethereal quality and condensing down to normal characters. The first word on the right for evening time is spread and stretched. The character for tea is dancing above the pattern playfully.

I close my eyes and try to intuitively sense the meaning. I see an archetypal oriental face and at the same time feel a playful whirling. Evening seems to be more than the evening of the day. It is also the evening time of life. The playful quality suggests that at the evening time of life we can experience vitality and youth. I express what I am finding to Masa: "With the wisdom of age comes youth. If we can keep our youth with age, we find wisdom." This seems to be the gift of the Tea Spirit. Green Tea is becoming known to have powerful anti-oxidant, anti-ageing properties. This is intriguing. Is this the gift of the tea spirit? To take us into old age, preserving our youth so that we can be wise? Are the playful animals, the health-giving gifts of green tea and the pursuit of Buddhist wisdom all connected?

I follow an intuition and, climbing a wall, find the tea growing area on the other side. The bushes are about waist height and have the same foliage colour and shape as small orange leaves.

We walk back to the main temple, where I wash the remains of midges out of my eyes in water piped through bamboo and a leaf into a hollowed stone. We take a bus back towards Kyoto where we will eat in a temple.

This is one temple in an extensive area containing many gardens and temples. We are seated in a garden with the bright sunshine broken up by the leaves of beautiful Japanese maples. We start with delicious frothy green tea. This time, I do the rotating of the bowl as before, but spend a little longer on the honouring. Masa tells me I needn't take so long!

We eat a delicious and delicate, vegetarian meal. I play with a three or four-year-old Japanese girl who is singing English nursery rhymes. "Heads and shoulders, knees and toes..."

As we leave the restaurant, we soon pass another temple gate. It is not in Masa's plan, but we decide to go in. It is interesting and beautiful, with a Zen garden of raked white gravel and rocks, but something else catches our attention.

The son of an early head of the temple had become a Christian in a Franciscan order. Seeing his father, choosing to fight wars for gain while still a monk, had disillusion him. The son had left Buddhism to follow Christianity because it was not tarnished in the same way. This is another example of someone crossing over between religions and of people losing their trust and faith in the religion of their upbringing. The same theme is repeating again. It feels as though we are being given the same message again and again.

We see more beautiful temples and gardens and end with dinner at a restaurant specialising in eel.

Return to Tokyo

That night, as we return to Tokyo on the Shinkansen, we are both quite tired.

I am checked into my new hotel in Tokyo by about midnight.

The next morning, Monday, we meet at about 9 – my latest start so far.

Our first meeting is with one of the large consultancies, organised with someone from the Japanese Balanced Scorecard Forum. We meet the person from the Balanced Scorecard Forum, someone in knowledge management and someone in government consulting. We share our government transformation experience and they offer a deeper insight into the same challenges of modernising government in Japan. The meeting is warm and positive. Somehow Masa has found great people to work with. I thank him.

The next meeting is with another person from the Forum who works for one of our global customers. It is great to see how news of our products and a positive reputation had already reached the other side of the planet.

Finally, we meet with a systems integration and data warehouse company. They already have an event planned to present our Balanced Scorecard product and love what we show of the web version. Together, we realise that with a focus on improving an organisation, quality, strategic control and IT, people can work together. It's a great message for a data warehouse vendor.

That evening, I meet the person who has done the technical work on translation of our products. He's done a good job.

Masa and I eat with his children at an Irish Bar – so that I can explain to the children what the different foods are. Masa translates when needed. I explain that I am not Irish, but I'll do my best! Masa's children are lovely. We play, translate and mime. The restaurant service is surprisingly bad – they forget to bring Masa's food entirely. The food is undoubtedly the worst we have eaten since in Japan, but the company is great.

We drop off the children and Masa takes me back to my hotel. We talk about food and health. I thank Masa for sharing his culture with me. He drops me at the hotel. After a paper-thin pizza in the Irish bar, where bacon was substituted for the Salmon I ordered, I still have an appetite. (I don't eat bacon!) After wandering for a while, I find a hidden something. Is it a bar? A restaurant? I go in. They serve food. I mull over the week's experiences. The man next to me at the counter speaks excellent English. He can't believe that I have found this all-Japanese eating-place. He gives me his perspective on the political situation and tells me about venture capital in Japan.

The next morning is Tuesday. I've been here a week and I'm flying home today. I meet Masa for breakfast and spend some time talking about pricing. We say a warm goodbye.

On the bus to the airport a final question is answered.

I stand up to get my passport from my pocket. The bus driver shouts at me. A paradox of Japanese culture is that on the one hand people are incredibly polite and on the other hand they can seem harsh. It seems that when you are on the right side of the rules you experience the politeness. When you break them, you should not expect to be tolerated. It is probably much easier for a Westerner too. We don't know the rules. A comment of Masa's comes to mind. Historically, Japan has had limited space. In the past, if your local community rejected you, there was nowhere to go so you had to fit in to survive. This mentality creates a fear of being different, of not fitting in. It creates a desire for compliance.

When I say I feel I need to learn Japanese, Masa says, "you don't need to, you've got me" I realise how lucky I am to have such a friend and colleague. I have been lucky to have Masa guiding me and we have been lucky having coincidence guiding both of us through experiences and ideas. I am grateful to have experienced and learned a lot in a short time. I leave with a love for this complex country and its people.

I have learned from my friend and mentor Richard Barrett that fear limits possibilities in people, organisations and nations. I hope that Japanese organisations will not choose to follow the lowest common denominator of global business culture. I feel a great optimism for what Japan can achieve by taking its traditional wisdom and applying it to the challenges that seem to face nations, governments and businesses around the world. Japan can lead the way in the global transformation that is forcing itself on all of us. Japanese organisations can take great strength from the deep cultural knowledge of kaizen, quality and environmental stewardship, but I suspect that people and organisations will need to let go of some fears from the past, to be able to grasp the opportunities of the twenty-first century.

On the aeroplane I take the green tea option rather than tea or coffee. I notice that I will never feel quite the same about green tea again.

Web links for this diary on WWW.MindOfMany.COM.

III. Personal Diet Practices

My diet and exercise practices affect my ability to think clearly, to be intuitive, loving and compassionate. As a simple example, if I drink alcohol and get a hangover, I am short-tempered. Over the last 20 years, I have refined my diet and exercise practices, most recently through learning with my partner Gina Lazenby who writes on the subject of health. The following table shows some of the substitutions we make for more conventional foods in our household.

Different people with different constitutions in different climates and cultures want and need different things. This is not a prescription for anyone else. It is a collection of habits that work for us at the moment and will change over time. I share it as example of the result of focusing on what works for me, rather than assuming that these habits are optimal for anyone else.

Replace	With
White bread, pasta, rice, etc.	Organic brown (whole grain) bread, pasta, rice, etc.
Fruit and vegetables	Organic fruit and vegetables
Processed, chilled, pre-packaged and frozen foods containing chemicals and additives	Fresh prepared foods from fresh organic ingredients where possible
Tea	Organic Rooibos Tea, Green Tea, Sliced Ginger and Hot Water (morning), Camomile Tea (Evening)
Coffee	Grain or Guarana Coffee
Traditional, continental or cereal breakfast	Smoothie made by liquidising for example spirulina, Cold Pressed Organic Flax Oil, an Organic

	Apple or Pear and spring water. Alternately, or followed by organic porridge or cereal with rice milk or soya milk an hour or more later.
Colas, Soft Drinks (Classic and Diet)	Water or drinks not sweetened with cane sugar or artificial additives
Sugar	Concentrated Apple Juice, Rice Malt Syrup, Maple Syrup, or other natural sweetener not derived from cane sugar
Salt and stock cubes	Organic Soya Sauce, Organic Miso, Organic Vegetable Stock Cubes. Kombu or Wakame seaweed added to rice and soups.
Tap or bottled water	Magnetic filtered water or spring water treated with PiMag filter or drops.
Chemical soaps and shampoos	Alternatives not containing Sodium Lauryl Sulphate or Sodium Laureth Sulphate (Faith in Nature)
Chemical household cleaning products	Natural eco-friendly (and hence person friendly) alternatives (Ecover)
Dishwasher Powder	Magnetic Wash Ball (reduces or replaces detergent)
Washing Powder	Magnetic Laundry Ball (reduces or replaces detergent)
Chemical paints and artificial or non-organic upholstery and carpets	Natural and organic alternatives

IV. Index to Part 1: Purpose and Vision

Afflictive emotions
   acting from **33**, **124**
   and peace of mind......33
   and serving purpose ...30
   choice in reaction33, 123
   comparing angry child...........................62
   definition...................**29**
   feedback.....................49
   gift in 48
   learning from **48**
   stopping acting from ..55
   to free our selves........30
   why work on them? ...48
Afflictive Emotions
   Freeze-Framer............36
   HeartMath..................**36**
African Excellence Model 81
Anger
   letting go of........**56**, **135**
Baby rabbits with REGs..**ix**
Beautiful garden
   of my mind...........**37, 69**
Billiard ball
   defining the mechanistic world view 5
   paradigm applied to life............................32
Body
   de-stressing habits......**59**
Boundaries
   garden of my mind.....38
   protecting...................49
   reinforce or heal.......130

Butterfly wing................. 8
   and intuitiion 11
   change the world 96
   makes a difference..... 10
   responsibility............. 66
CareGiver 39
CareTaker 38
Chakras......................... 28
Chaos Theory 8
Chicks with REGs .... **ix**
Committed
   Until one is... 66
Compassion xiv
   and building perfection 53
   and getting back on the mark...................... 72
   and Heisenberg.......... 78
   and karma.................. 69
   and knowing ourselves.................... 79
   and knowledge **78**
   and meaning in forgiveness 131
   and suffering.............. 72
   and understanding 79
   developing................. **78**
   for enemies................ 83
   from non-judgement.. 79
   in organisations 80
   perceiving with.......... 76
CPA 82
Dalai Lama 30
David Bohm viii
Debris
   in the body................. **44**

in the mind 40
destiny 12
EFQM 81
EFT
   Emotional Freedom Technique **34**
Eggs x
Einstein 7
Emerging Global Transformation **4**
   awsome beautiful pattern **21**
Fireflies 186
Forgive **54**
Forgiveness xiv, 137, 140, 141
   as a step towards freedom 54
   eroding ability to manifest 49
   the gift of **54**
   to clean up and complete 34
Fractal 179
Free will **54**
   reclaiming 29
Freeze-Framer 35
Fruit fly larvae x
Gandhi 43, 62
Gauge state x
George Bernard Shaw quote 12
Global Consciousness Project x
GPRA 82
Green Tea 188
Guilt
   letting go of **56, 134**
HeartMath **35**

Heisenberg
   and compassion 78
   and electrons 68
   Uncertainty Principle 7, **68**
Hiroshima 180
Idea That Changed the World i
Implicate Order
   affecting 75
   and causative acts **67**
   intention **65**
   synchronicity **65**
Inner certainty xv
Intention
   affects reality .... **x**
Internal Heaven
   and building perfection 53
   and manifesting our dreams 53
   by changing our minds 53
Intuition **11, 19**
   4 steps for **22**
   choosing 11
   nurturing **22**
Japan 175
Japan Quality Awards 81
Kaizen 174
Kanji 178
Karma
   a law like gravity **71**
   love and the Implicate Order 75
   Newton's Laws 68
   positive 69
   the gift of free tuition. **67**
   Universal gravity 72
Knowledge

and compassion 78
Kozan-Ji 187
Kundalini Yoga **28**, 60
Kyoto 183
Liver enzyme x
Love .... xiv, **75**
   and karma 76
   love your enemy 83
   surrender to 77
Lynn McTaggart viii
Magnetic
   alignment 85
   purpose and vision 85
Mahatma Gandhi 43
Malcolm Baldridge 81
Manifest **49**
Marianne Williamson ... 107
Mechanistic
   world view 5
Meditation
   Breath **28**, **122**
   Exercises **120**
Meditators x
Meridian
   Kundalini Yoga 28
Midas 75
Mind
   beautiful garden of **37**
   care
      giving up worry **61**
      de-stressing habits **60**
Miracles
   familiarity with 66
nature
   honouring 188
Nelson Mandela ... 106, 186
New Science 8
New World 102
Newton 5

cause and effect 67
cradle 5
laws of mechanics 4
over using his laws 32
spiritual interpretation 68
Third Law 67
Non-violence 43
Observe-Orient-Decide-
   Act 82
Off the mark **18**
Old World 101
On the mark **18**
   getting back 31
OODA Loop 82, 173
Partners
   in vision 93
PDCA 174
Peace of mind
   Exercises **24**
   reclaiming **137**
Performance Management
   .... 82, 184
Perpetrator 38
Peter Senge 7
pH x
Plan-Do-Check-Act 174
Purpose .... xiv, **11**
   discover your 113
   power of 13
   statistic 13
   true joy in life 11
   used by a mighty one. 12
Random Event Generator
   .... **viii**
Reacting
   choice **33**, **123**
   from afflictive
      emotion **33**
REG .... **viii**, **x**

René Peoc'h ix
Repentance
    Zen Archer 17
Roger Nelson xi
Saint Francis of Assisi 180, 187
September 11th 2001 xiii
    Consciousness xii
Sin
    Zen Archer 17
South Africa Performance Management 5
Stillness **24**
Stress 58, 59
    adrenaline 59
    and adrenaline 46
    and free will........... 40, 47
    and good judgement .. 58
    and healing 44
    and love and compassion 40
    and pain 45
    and peace of mind 24
    and staying on the mark 41
    and Suffering Cycle... 41
    elimination
        Body care habits **59**
        Body intake habits . **58**
        Giving up worry **61**

Mind de-stressing habits **60**
    freedom from **58**
    from damaged boundaries 40
    in leaders 8
    pushed by 2
    vigorous exercise 60
Suffering
    as fuel for commitment 53
Suffering Cycle **40**
Synchronicity
    and the Implicate Order 65
tea ceremony 188
Tea Spirit 189
The Field viii
Transforming Cycle **41**
Victim 38
Vision 99
    emerging **83**
    pulled by 2
    shared 92
    tidal pull of 15
William Tiller (Dr) .... **x**
Yin and Yang 181
Zen 177
Zen Archer
    aligning with purpose **17, 70**